PAT BROWN, MBA

CheerMoney101

Using Cheer to Teach the Basics of Money

AF808157

ABRAM · 47 · BROWN

First published by AbramBrown47 2026

First edition

ISBN: 978-1-967737-51-2

This book was professionally typeset on Reedsy.
Find out more at reedsy.com

Contents

Foreword

Cheerleading is built on trust, timing, and precision.

Every count matters. Every motion has a purpose. Every athlete depends on the person next to them to do their job exactly when and how they are supposed to. When even one piece is off, the entire routine feels it.

Money works the same way.

Most athletes never receive a clear financial playbook. They train relentlessly for competition, yet are expected to figure out finances on their own once the routine ends. Bills, contracts, taxes, savings, and long-term planning arrive without counts, coaches, or clear expectations.

This book exists to change that.

Cheer Money 101 was written for current and former cheerleaders who understand discipline, repetition, and teamwork, but may not have been taught how those same principles apply to money. It does not assume prior financial knowledge. It assumes you know what it means to prepare, to trust the process, and to perform under pressure.

Cheerleading teaches lessons that translate perfectly to financial stability. You learn that rushing leads to mistakes. You learn that consistency beats perfection. You learn that safety, structure, and communication protect everyone involved. Those same truths apply to building a stable financial life.

This book is not about shortcuts or flashy wins. It is about clean execution. It is about showing up, hitting your counts, and building habits that hold when life gets busy or unpredictable. Financial success, like a strong routine, is the result of many small actions done correctly over time.

The goal is not to overwhelm you. The goal is to give you clarity, confidence, and structure. Just like cheer, when you understand the counts and trust your teammates, the routine starts to feel manageable.

The responsibility does not end when the routine does.

This book helps you carry what cheer taught you into the rest of your life.

Introduction

At some point, the music stops.

The routine ends. The mat clears. The crowd reacts. Win or lose, the performance is over. For cheerleaders, that moment comes suddenly. One season you are training daily with a team, coaches, and clear expectations. The next, the structure is gone.

What does not end is responsibility.

Life after cheer does not come with counts, music cues, or judges' sheets. There is no one telling you when to save, when to plan, or how to protect yourself financially. Yet the consequences of those decisions are real and long lasting.

This is where many former athletes struggle.

Cheer teaches discipline, repetition, trust, and attention to detail. But financial literacy is rarely taught alongside those skills. Most cheerleaders leave the sport highly capable, highly disciplined, and completely unprepared for money decisions that begin immediately after competition ends.

The transition feels subtle at first.

A paycheck instead of a stipend.

Bills instead of team fees.

Choices instead of instructions.

Without realizing it, the responsibility shifts from the team to you.

This book is not about replacing cheer. It is about translating what cheer already taught you. The same skills that helped you stay in sync with a routine are the ones that help you build financial stability. Timing matters. Consistency matters. Trusting the process matters.

Mistakes in cheer are immediate. Miss a count and everyone sees it. Money mistakes are delayed. Overspending today shows up as stress later. Skipping planning now limits options years down the road. The absence of immediate feedback makes financial responsibility harder, not easier.

Cheer Money 101 exists to close that gap.

It gives you structure when structure disappears. It gives you language for decisions that were never explained. It helps you understand how to move forward when the routine ends but life keeps going.

The responsibility continues whether you are ready or not.

This book helps you be ready.

About This Book

Cheerleading is not chaos.

From the outside, routines may look fast and complex, but every movement is planned. Every count is intentional. Every stunt, transition, and landing is built on preparation, trust, and repetition. When cheer is done well, it looks effortless. When fundamentals are missed, everything falls apart.

Money works the same way.

Financial stability is not about luck or perfection. It is about timing, consistency, and clean execution. The principles that make a cheer routine successful are the same principles that build a strong financial life.

This book is built on that connection.

Cheer teaches you that rushing creates mistakes. In money, rushing leads to bad decisions. Cheer teaches you that skipping reps shows up under pressure. In money, skipping planning shows up later as stress. Cheer teaches you that safety and structure protect the entire team. In money, protection and preparation do the same.

Cheer Money 101 uses cheerleading language, situations, and mindset to explain personal finance in a way that feels familiar. There is no jargon. No assumptions that you have studied finance. The goal is to make money feel structured instead of overwhelming.

This book is organized like a season.

You will start with fundamentals. Understanding where you are, how money flows, and how to build consistency. From there, the focus shifts to safety, protection, and longevity. Later sections address balance, long-term planning, and life beyond the mat.

Each chapter connects a financial concept to a cheer concept you already understand. Counts become timing. Trust becomes discipline. Safety becomes protection. Reps become habits. Teamwork becomes shared responsibility.

This book does not promise perfection.

It promises clarity.

You do not need to execute every move flawlessly. You need to show up, hit your counts, and trust the process. Financial stability is built the same way routines are built, one clean rep at a time.

Cheer already taught you how to do hard things together.

This book shows you how to apply those lessons to money.

Foolish Assumptions

Every rule book starts with assumptions.

So does this one.

Not because assumptions are perfect, but because pretending everyone starts in the same place creates confusion. This section clarifies what *Cheer Money 101* assumes about you, your experience, and your mindset so the rest of the book makes sense.

Some of these assumptions may fit you exactly. Some may not. That is okay.

This Book Assumes You Understand Discipline

If you have competed in cheer, you understand discipline.

You know what it means to show up when you are tired. To repeat the same skill until it is clean. To trust the process even when progress feels slow. You understand that effort is expected, not celebrated.

This book assumes you can apply that same discipline to money once you understand the system.

This Book Assumes You Are Used to Structure

Cheer is structured.

Counts matter. Timing matters. Roles matter. The routine works because everyone knows where to be and when to be there.

This book assumes that structure makes you more comfortable, not less. The goal is not to overwhelm you with options. The goal is to give you a routine for your finances.

This Book Assumes You May Not Have Been Taught Financial Basics

This is a big one.

Most athletes are never formally taught how money works. Not budgeting. Not investing. Not taxes. Not protection. That is not a failure on your part.

This book assumes you are capable and motivated, even if you were never given the instruction.

This Book Assumes You Care About Long-Term Stability

Cheer teaches you to think beyond one count.

Safety, consistency, and trust are about protecting the entire routine, not just one moment. This book assumes you want that same stability in your life.

Not quick wins. Not shortcuts. Stability.

This Book Assumes You Are Willing to Be Honest With Yourself

Progress requires honesty.

Cheer demands self-awareness. You know when something is off. You know when you skipped reps. Money requires the same honesty.

This book assumes you are willing to look at your habits without judgment and make adjustments when needed.

What This Book Does Not Assume

It does not assume you are perfect.

It does not assume you are rich.

It does not assume you have everything figured out.

It does not assume you want complexity.

It assumes you are coachable.

Why These Assumptions Matter

If these assumptions are mostly true, this book will feel familiar. If they are not, that is okay. The structure will still help.

Just like cheer, growth happens when you commit to the process.

Athlete Takeaways

- Discipline is already a skill you have.
- Structure supports consistency.
- Not being taught money is not a failure.
- Long-term stability beats quick wins.
- Honesty is the starting point for improvement.

How This Playbook Is Organized

Cheer routines are not built all at once.

They start with basics. Counts. Timing. Motions. From there, difficulty increases. Skills are layered. Transitions are refined. The routine only works because each phase builds on the one before it.

This playbook is organized the same way.

Cheer Money 101 is designed to move in a logical sequence so you are never asked to perform skills you have not practiced yet. Each part builds structure, confidence, and understanding before moving forward.

Part I: Counts, Timing, and Fundamentals

This section establishes your foundation.

You will learn how to understand where you are financially, how money flows in and out, and how to build consistency through budgeting, saving, and basic banking. These chapters focus on awareness and control.

If the basics are off, nothing else works. Just like cheer, fundamentals come first.

Part II: Safety, Protection, and Longevity

Cheer prioritizes safety before difficulty.

This section focuses on risk, insurance, and protection. You will learn how to protect yourself from financial injuries that can derail progress and limit future options.

Longevity matters. The goal is not to survive one season. It is to stay in the game long term.

Part III: Balance, Control, and Long-Term Stability

Once fundamentals and protection are in place, balance becomes the focus.

This section covers investing, asset allocation, discipline, and mental resilience. It explains how to build stability without overcomplicating decisions and how to stay composed when pressure increases.

Balance keeps routines clean and portfolios steady.

Part IV: Life Beyond the Mat

Cheer ends. Life continues.

This section addresses taxes, careers, housing, family responsibilities, and major life decisions. These chapters focus on applying financial discipline to real-world situations that extend far beyond athletics.

Part V: Finishing Strong Together

The final section focuses on long-term success.

You will learn how to build the right support system, avoid scams, and stay disciplined over time. Winning beyond the mat requires teamwork, trust, and consistency.

How to Use This Book

You can read this book cover to cover or return to specific sections as needed. Like a routine, repetition matters. Revisiting chapters strengthens understanding.

This playbook is not meant to be rushed.

Hit your counts.

Trust the process.

Build stability one rep at a time.

About Pat Brown

Pat Brown played college football at the University of Kansas from 1994 to 1999 and was named team captain for the 1999 season. His years in the locker room shaped his views on accountability, discipline, preparation, and leadership, principles that continue to guide his work long after football.

Following his playing career, Pat transitioned into financial services and built a career as a financial advisor and wealth manager. He works with individuals, families, business owners, and athletes navigating increasingly complex financial lives. He pursued advanced education and professional development, earning an MBA along with industry designations including ChFC®, RICP®, and CAP®. His background blends academic training with real-world experience in financial planning, retirement income strategies, tax planning, and philanthropy.

As the college sports landscape changed with the introduction of Name, Image, and Likeness opportunities, Pat recognized a growing education gap. Student athletes were gaining access to income, contracts, and endorsements without the financial knowledge needed to manage taxes, cash flow, business structures, and long-term consequences. That reality became the catalyst for his work in the NIL space.

Pat has since become a recognized voice in athlete financial education and has been interviewed by national publications and platforms including Financial Planning, Yahoo, and ESPN Andscape, where he shares insights on NIL planning, financial literacy gaps, and the challenges facing student athletes and their families.

These experiences led Pat to author a series of practical, athlete-focused books designed to meet athletes and families where they are. His NIL-related titles include *Financial Literacy for NIL*, *Financial Literacy for NIL for Parents of Student Athletes, Financial Literacy for NIL for High School Students,* and *Financial Literacy for NIL for International Student Athletes.* Each book is written to be clear, accessible, and grounded in real-world scenarios rather than theory.

Pat also created a growing collection of sport-specific financial education titles, including *Football Money 101, Baseball Money 101, Basketball Money 101, Cheer Money 101, Dance Money 101, Gymnastics Money 101, Hockey Money 101, Lacrosse Money 101, Rowing Money 101, Soccer Money 101, Softball Money 101, Tennis Money 101, Track Money 101, Volleyball Money 101,* and *Wrestling Money 101.* Each book translates the culture, discipline, and mindset of the sport into financial lessons athletes can apply long after competition ends.

To extend this mission beyond books, Pat founded Former Student Athlete, a platform created to support athletes navigating life after sports. Former Student Athlete provides education, community, and real-world resources focused on financial literacy, career transitions, health, identity, and long-term success once the uniform comes off. His broader education platforms can be found at www.formerstudentathlete.com, www.financialliteracyfornil.com, www.financialliteracyforstudentathletes.com, and www.parentsofstudentathletes.com.

Pat is easy to find through a Google search, on LinkedIn, or on Twitter, where he regularly shares insights on athletes, money, and life after sports. If you would like to visit with Pat specifically about Cheer *Money 101,* you can reach him directly at info@cheermoney101.com.

Pat's work is rooted in a belief shaped by both football and finance. Athletes deserve a better playbook for life after sports, and financial education should arrive before opportunity turns into regret.

Part I: Counts, Timing, and Fundamentals

If the basics are off, the entire routine falls apart.

Every strong cheer routine starts the same way. Long before stunts, baskets, or full-out performances, there are counts. Timing. Sharp motions practiced again and again until they are second nature. Teams do not skip this stage, no matter how talented they are. They drill fundamentals because they know one simple truth: when the basics are clean, everything else has a chance to work. When they are not, even the most skilled athletes struggle to stay in sync.

Money works exactly the same way.

Most financial stress does not come from complex investing strategies, tax loopholes, or advanced planning decisions. It comes from basics that were never built or were ignored over time. Not knowing where money is going each month. Saving inconsistently. Carrying high-interest debt without a plan. Letting credit habits slide. Living without a structure that creates rhythm and control.

You cannot layer difficulty on top of instability.

Just like in cheer, you cannot expect to hit elite-level skills if your counts are off or your motions are sloppy. The routine may look fine for a moment, but eventually it breaks down. The same thing happens with money. People try to jump straight to investing, home ownership, or big lifestyle upgrades without first establishing control over cash flow and habits. When something unexpected happens, a missed paycheck, an emergency expense, a life change, everything starts to wobble.

This first part of the book is about establishing rhythm and control.

It is about understanding how money flows in and out of your life. Learning to track it, direct it, and manage it with intention. It is about building habits that hold up even when life gets busy, stressful, or unpredictable. These are the financial equivalents of clean motions and consistent counts. They may not feel exciting, but they are what make everything else possible.

These chapters are not flashy. They are essential.

They focus on awareness, structure, and consistency. They help you build confidence because you know what your money is doing and why. They reduce mistakes because decisions are no longer made on impulse or panic. They allow you to progress without constantly having to reset, recover, or clean up financial messes from the past.

In cheer, teams that rush through fundamentals spend the rest of the season fixing the same problems. Teams that commit to the basics early move faster later. They trust each other. They trust the routine. They perform with confidence instead of fear.

Your financial life is no different.

If you rush past this part, the routine breaks later. You may still succeed for a while, but it will feel fragile and stressful. If you commit to it, everything that follows becomes easier to manage. Investing decisions make more sense. Big goals feel achievable. Setbacks are less overwhelming because you have a foundation to fall back on.

This is where stability begins.

Chapter 1: Why Money Feels Confusing After Cheer

Cheer is precise.

Counts are clear. Timing is defined. Coaches tell you exactly what needs to happen and when. If something is off, you feel it immediately. The music does not wait. Your teammates do not wait. The routine either hits or it does not. Feedback is instant and obvious, and corrections happen in real time.

Money is the opposite.

After cheer, there is no music cue telling you when to save. No judge's sheet highlighting missed counts. No coach pulling you aside to correct habits before they become problems. Bills get paid or they do not. Debt quietly grows. Savings slowly disappear. Often, you do not realize something is wrong until the consequences are already in motion.

The lack of structure is why money feels confusing, even for disciplined athletes.

Why Financial Literacy Is Rarely Taught to Athletes

Most athletes are trained to perform, not to plan financially.

From a young age, time is devoted to conditioning, technique, safety, and competition. Practices are scheduled. Expectations are clear. Progress is measured. Financial education, however, is usually treated as someone else's responsibility. Parents are expected to teach it. Schools are assumed to cover it. Life later on is supposed to sort it out.

The result is predictable.

Athletes often leave cheer with strong discipline, high work ethic, and the ability to handle pressure, yet with little understanding of how money actually works. That is not a personal failure. It is a system gap.

In cheer terms, it is like being asked to perform a routine without ever being taught counts. You might have strength and flexibility, but without structure, everything feels rushed and out of sync.

Money Myths Passed Through Gyms and Squads

Just like cheer, money myths spread informally.

They are rarely taught in a classroom. They are overheard in conversations, picked up from teammates, family members, or social media. Over time, they become accepted as truth.

You hear things like:

Saving is only for people who make a lot of money.

Investing is too risky.

You will figure it out later.

As long as the bills are paid, everything is fine.

These ideas are rarely questioned. They sound reasonable on the surface, so they stick.

In cheer terms, this is learning technique from teammates instead of coaches. Sometimes you get lucky. Often, bad habits form and go uncorrected until they limit progress or cause injury. Financial myths work the same way. They feel harmless at first, but they quietly create instability over time.

Saving vs Investing vs Gambling

This is where confusion often increases.

Saving, investing, and gambling are three very different actions, but without education, they can blur together.

Saving is about safety and stability. It is there to protect you from unexpected falls. Emergencies, car repairs, medical bills, and short-term needs live here. Saving does not need to be exciting. It needs to be reliable.

Investing is about long-term growth. It requires patience, consistency, and a plan. The goal is not quick wins. It is steady progress over time, accepting that there will be ups and downs along the way.

Gambling is chasing outcomes without a plan. It is emotional. It is reactive. It is driven by excitement, fear, or the desire to make up for lost time.

Many people confuse these three because no one explains the difference. They save too little because it feels slow. They invest emotionally and panic at normal market movement. Or they gamble without realizing it, calling it investing when it is really just guessing.

In cheer terms:

Saving is your mat and spotters.

Investing is the season-long training plan.

Gambling is throwing a skill you have not practiced.

Each has a role. Mixing them up creates unnecessary risk.

Why Consistency Beats Chasing Perfect Routines

Cheer routines are not built on perfection.

They are built on repetition. Clean counts. Consistent execution. One mistake does not end a season. Repeated mistakes do. Teams that succeed are not the ones who never mess up. They are the ones who correct quickly and keep showing up prepared.

Money works the same way.

You do not need perfect financial decisions. You need consistent ones. Saving a small amount regularly beats waiting for the perfect moment to start. Investing steadily beats trying to time every move exactly right. Paying attention to habits matters more than finding the one perfect strategy.

Chasing perfection delays progress. Consistency builds stability.

A Coach's Perspective

A coach would say it simply.

Hit your counts.

Do the basics.

Stop overthinking.

Trust the process.

Money rewards repetition, not perfection. The people who succeed financially are rarely the ones making brilliant moves all the time. They are the ones doing simple things well, over and over, even when it feels boring.

Game Situations and Decision Points

Just like competition, money presents moments that test decision-making.

You feel behind. Do you rush, or do you stay consistent?

You hear conflicting advice. Do you question it, or accept it without understanding?

You make a mistake. Do you quit, or do you correct and move forward?

These moments may seem small, but they shape outcomes over time. One rushed decision rarely ruins everything, but repeated rushed decisions do. One mistake does not define you. Refusing to adjust does.

Common Athlete Mistakes and Financial Parallels

Athletes rush skills when they feel pressure. Financially, that leads to impulsive decisions and unnecessary risk.

Athletes copy bad habits when they do not know better. Financially, that turns myths into truth and keeps people stuck.

Athletes avoid fundamentals because they feel boring or basic. Financially, that creates instability and stress when life gets unpredictable.

The parallels are clear once you see them.

Winning the Long Game

Money feels confusing because the structure disappeared, not because you are incapable.

Athletes already understand discipline, repetition, and delayed gratification. What is missing is a framework. Once the basics are clear, everything slows down. Decisions feel less emotional. Progress becomes visible. Confidence grows.

Just like cheer, clarity brings confidence.

Athlete Takeaways

Money confusion comes from lack of structure, not lack of ability.

Financial myths spread when fundamentals are missing.

Saving, investing, and gambling are not the same thing.

Consistency matters more than perfection.

Hit your counts. Do the basics. Keep moving forward.

Chapter 2: Check the Counts: Your Financial Snapshot

Before any routine runs full out, you check the counts.

You walk through the timing. You make sure everyone knows where they are supposed to be. You do not guess. You do not assume. You confirm. If the counts are off at the beginning, everything downstream feels rushed and unstable. Skills that normally feel easy start to feel forced. Timing slips. Confidence drops. The routine does not fall apart because the team is not talented. It falls apart because the foundation was never checked.

Your finances work the same way.

A financial snapshot is simply checking your counts. It is not about judgment. It is about awareness. You cannot fix what you refuse to look at, and you cannot improve what you do not measure. Most people do not fail financially because they are irresponsible. They struggle because they are running full out without ever doing a walkthrough.

A snapshot is a pause. A reset. A moment to see what is actually true, not what you hope is true.

Income, Expenses, and Cash Flow

Income is what comes in.

Expenses are what go out.

Cash flow is the difference.

That sounds simple, but many people never actually calculate it. They know they are "getting by," but they do not know why, and they do not know how tight the margin really is. They cannot tell you how much is left after essentials, or how much of their money is already spoken for before it even hits their account.

In cheer terms, cash flow is timing.

Even if your income looks fine on paper, stress increases when timing is off. If your paycheck hits after bills are due, everything feels harder. You might have enough money overall, but the mismatch creates late fees, overdrafts, and constant pressure. It is like being one count behind all the way through the routine. You are still moving, but you are chasing the music instead of leading it.

Positive cash flow creates flexibility. Negative cash flow creates pressure.

The goal is not perfection. The goal is clarity. When you know your cash flow, you can make decisions with your eyes open instead of reacting at the last second.

Assets, Liabilities, and Net Worth

Assets are what you own.

Liabilities are what you owe.

Net worth is the difference.

This is not a scorecard of success. It is a starting point.

Many athletes avoid this step because it feels intimidating. If debt exists, it feels like failure. If savings are low, it can feel discouraging. But ignoring it does not make it better. It just hides problems until they grow. You cannot outwork what you will not face.

In cheer terms, this is knowing your base.

If your foundation is weak, you do not add difficulty. You do not try a more complex stunt to "make up for it." You stabilize first. You build strength. You clean technique. You make sure your base is solid enough to hold what comes next.

Net worth is a snapshot, not a verdict.

It will change as your habits change. The point is not to impress anyone. The point is to know where you stand so you can move forward with intention.

Fixed vs Variable Expenses

Fixed expenses stay mostly the same. Rent. Insurance. Subscriptions.

Variable expenses change. Food. Gas. Entertainment. Shopping.

Most people focus on income and ignore expenses. That is backwards. In the short term, you often have more control over expenses than income. You may not be able to increase your paycheck overnight, but you can usually reduce leaks and create breathing room faster than you think.

In cheer terms, fixed expenses are your required counts.

They are the pieces of the routine that must happen. You cannot skip them. Variable expenses are optional motions. When things feel tight, you do not start by cutting the required counts. You clean up the optional motions first.

Understanding this distinction gives you leverage.

It shows you what is locked in and what is flexible. It helps you avoid the trap of thinking you are "bad with money" when the real problem is that too much is committed before you even get a chance to choose.

Reviewing Where Your Money Actually Goes

This is the most important part.

Not where you think your money goes. Where it actually goes.

Bank statements and credit card statements tell the truth. Patterns appear quickly once you look. Small leaks add up. Convenience spending becomes routine spending. Subscriptions you forgot about quietly renew. Food spending slowly climbs because it is easier to swipe a card than to plan ahead. None of this makes you a failure. It makes you human.

In cheer terms, this is film study.

The film does not lie. You might feel like the routine is clean, but the video shows the real timing. It shows the bobble in the stunt. It shows the late motion. It shows the spacing issue you did not notice in the moment.

Statements are financial film.

They show what is happening when you are not paying attention. And once you see it, you can fix it. Awareness creates control.

Coach's Perspective

A coach would slow you down here.

Check the counts.

Know your starting position.

Do not rush ahead.

Clean first, then build.

You do not fix timing by guessing. You do not fix a routine by "trying harder" without knowing what is off. You fix it by identifying the issue, correcting it, and repeating the basics until the correction becomes automatic.

Money is the same.

If you are overwhelmed, the answer is rarely a complicated strategy. The answer is usually a clearer snapshot and a cleaner set of habits.

Game Situations and Decision Points

This is where it gets real.

You are afraid to look. Do you avoid it or face it?

You see something off. Do you ignore it or adjust?

You want progress fast. Do you build a foundation or skip steps?

These moments determine everything that follows.

Avoidance feels easier in the moment, but it costs you later. Facing the numbers may feel uncomfortable, but it gives you power. Once you know what is true, you can make a plan that actually works.

Common Athlete Mistakes and Financial Parallels

Athletes assume timing is fine. Financially, that leads to surprises.

Athletes skip walkthroughs. Financially, that leads to confusion.

Athletes rush difficulty. Financially, that leads to instability.

The pattern is consistent: when you skip the basics, you pay for it later.

Winning the Long Game

A clean routine starts with clear counts.

A stable financial life starts with a clear snapshot.

Once you know where you are, you can move forward with confidence. You can set goals that are realistic. You can fix what is off before it becomes a bigger issue. You can stop guessing and start leading.

Athlete Takeaways

Income, expenses, and cash flow show your timing.

Assets and liabilities define your foundation.

Fixed and variable expenses create leverage.

Statements tell the truth.

Check the counts before adding difficulty

Chapter 3: Hitting Every Count: Budgeting and Saving

Cheer routines do not survive on talent alone.

They survive on timing. On hitting every count exactly when it is supposed to happen. When someone rushes or lags, the entire routine feels off, even if no one crashes. Judges can see it. Teammates can feel it. The routine loses its confidence and control, not because the athletes lack ability, but because the rhythm is broken.

Budgeting and saving work the same way.

Most people think budgeting is restrictive. Athletes know better. Structure does not limit performance. It supports it. A good routine does not feel restrictive once you know it. It feels freeing. You stop guessing. You stop hesitating. You move with confidence because you know what comes next.

A good budget works the same way. It is not about saying no to everything. It is about knowing your counts so you can move forward without second guessing every decision.

Budgeting Systems That Actually Work

Budgets fail when they are too complicated.

Spreadsheets with dozens of categories. Apps that require constant attention. Rules that are unrealistic or too rigid. These systems break because they demand perfection, and perfection is not sustainable in real life. Miss one month, fall behind once, and the whole system gets abandoned.

What works is simple and repeatable.

Know what comes in.

Know what must go out.

Decide in advance where the rest goes.

That is it.

In cheer terms, this is a clean routine. You do not add extra motions just to look impressive. You hit what matters. You repeat it until it feels natural. A budget should feel like choreography you can run without dread, not a routine you avoid practicing.

The best budget is not the most detailed one. It is the one you can stick to consistently.

Automating Savings Like Daily Reps

Reps build consistency.

You do not rely on motivation to show up to practice. You rely on schedule. Practice happens whether you feel like it or not, and that consistency is what builds strength and confidence over time.

Automation does the same thing for saving.

Automatic transfers remove emotion from the process. Money moves before you have a chance to overthink it, justify skipping it, or convince yourself you will do it later. Saving becomes part of the routine instead of a monthly debate.

In cheer terms, this is muscle memory.

You do not consciously think through every motion once it is trained. You trust the reps. Automation allows your financial habits to work in the background, even when life gets busy or stressful.

Start small if needed. The amount matters far less than the consistency. Small, repeated actions compound over time in ways that feel almost invisible at first, then powerful later.

Emergency Funds as Injury Protection

Every athlete understands injury risk.

You train to reduce it. You condition properly. You warm up. You learn safety techniques. You do not expect injuries, but you respect the reality that they can happen.

Emergency funds serve the same purpose financially.

Unexpected expenses are not failures. They are part of life. Car repairs. Medical bills. Travel for family emergencies. Job changes. Without savings, these moments turn into crises. With savings, they become problems you can manage.

An emergency fund is not about growth. It is about protection.

In cheer terms, this is safety training. You hope you never need it, but when something goes wrong, it prevents serious damage. It keeps one bad moment from turning into a long recovery.

Balancing Lifestyle With Long-Term Goals

This is where many people struggle.

They believe saving means giving up everything fun. That mindset leads to burnout. Just like overtraining, extreme restriction works for a short time and then collapses. The goal is not deprivation. The goal is balance.

You can enjoy life now while preparing for later. That requires intentional choices instead of impulse spending. It means deciding what actually matters to you and letting the rest go without guilt.

In cheer terms, this is endurance.

You cannot go full out every count with maximum intensity and expect to finish strong. You pace yourself. You breathe where you can. You manage energy so the routine holds together from start to finish.

Money works the same way. Sustainable habits beat extreme ones every time.

Coach's Perspective

A coach would keep it simple.

Hit your counts.

Trust the reps.

Protect yourself.

Stay balanced.

No coach tells an athlete to perform without structure. No coach expects perfection every time. The expectation is consistency, effort, and adjustment when something is off.

Budgeting is about rhythm, not restriction.

Game Situations and Decision Points

This is where habits are tested.

You want something now. Do you check the plan or ignore it?

Saving feels small. Do you stay consistent or give up?

An emergency hits. Are you protected or scrambling?

These moments seem small on their own, but they compound quickly. Just like in cheer, what you do under pressure reveals whether the fundamentals are truly in place.

Common Athlete Mistakes and Financial Parallels

Athletes rush timing.

Financially, that leads to overspending.

Athletes skip reps.

Financially, that leads to inconsistency.

Athletes ignore safety.

Financially, that leads to stress and setbacks.

The pattern is clear. When fundamentals are skipped, consequences follow.

Winning the Long Game

Hitting every count creates confidence.

A consistent budget and steady saving do the same. You stop guessing. You stop reacting. You feel in control, even when life throws unexpected challenges your way.

You do not need perfection. You need rhythm. Over time, rhythm becomes stability.

Athlete Takeaways

Simple budgets are more effective than complex ones.

Automation builds consistency without effort.

Emergency funds protect against unexpected hits.

Balance prevents burnout.

Hit your counts and trust the routine.

Chapter 4: Credit, Debt, and Missed Counts

In cheer, missed counts do not always cause an immediate fall.

Sometimes the routine keeps moving. The music continues. From the outside, everything looks fine. The team hits the next stunt. The basket still goes up. No one crashes to the mat. But inside the routine, timing is no longer clean. One missed count forces small compensations. Someone rushes to catch up. Someone hesitates to avoid colliding. Spacing tightens. Breathing changes. Pressure builds quietly, even though the audience may not notice anything wrong.

Eventually, something gives.

Debt works the same way.

Credit and debt mistakes rarely create instant collapse. They are subtle at first. A balance that lingers longer than planned. A payment that arrives a few days late. A credit card used for convenience instead of intention. None of these moments feel dramatic on their own. Life keeps moving. Paychecks still come in. Bills still get paid. But timing is off, and that misalignment shows up later when pressure increases.

By the time debt becomes overwhelming, the routine has usually been unstable for a long time.

How Credit Scores and Reports Actually Work

Your credit report is a detailed record.

Your credit score is a simplified summary of that record.

The report tracks your behavior over time. It shows whether payments are made on time, how much you owe compared to your available credit, how long you have used credit, and how often you apply for new accounts. The score condenses all of that information into a single number used by lenders, landlords, insurers, and sometimes employers.

It is not a judgment of character.

It is not a measure of intelligence.

It is not a statement about effort or discipline in other areas of life.

It is a consistency and timing score.

In cheer terms, your credit score is your timing sheet. Clean reps raise it. Missed counts lower it. One late payment does not destroy everything. One mistake does not define you. Patterns matter. Repeated late payments, consistently high balances, or constant applications for new credit slowly throw off timing and lower the score.

Understanding this changes how credit feels.

Instead of something mysterious or intimidating, it becomes something measurable. You know what actions help and what actions hurt. Fear is replaced with control. Just like in cheer, once you understand the counts, you can clean them.

Credit Cards, Loans, and the Weight of Interest

Credit cards and loans are tools.

Used intentionally, they provide flexibility. They allow you to smooth cash flow, handle planned expenses, or invest in long term needs. Used without structure, they create drag. Interest is the cost of borrowing time. The longer money stays borrowed, the heavier it becomes.

In cheer terms, interest is fatigue.

One extra rep is manageable. You can push through it. But repeating bad reps over and over wears you down. Your form slips. Recovery takes longer. Eventually, even simple skills feel harder than they should.

Carrying balances works the same way financially. At first, minimum payments feel manageable. Over time, more and more effort goes toward staying in place instead of moving forward. Money that could have been used for saving or investing gets diverted to interest instead.

Paying attention to interest rates and balances is not about fear. It is about efficiency. You are protecting your energy and your future options. When interest is controlled, progress accelerates. When it is ignored, everything feels heavier.

Good Debt vs Bad Debt Is About Impact, Not Labels

Not all debt is the same.

Good debt supports long term stability or growth and fits within your budget. It is planned. It has a purpose. It does not force constant stress or sacrifice elsewhere. Bad debt creates pressure, limits options, and delivers short term satisfaction at long term cost.

In cheer terms, good debt is building strength safely. It supports the routine and prepares you for higher difficulty later. Bad debt is throwing skills you are not ready for. It might look exciting in the moment, but it increases the chance of injury and breakdown.

The difference is not the type of debt. It is the effect.

Does the debt give you flexibility or remove it?

Does it support stability or create constant tension?

Does it fit within your rhythm, or does it force you to rush and compensate?

Those questions matter far more than labels.

Debt Mistakes That Quietly Throw Off the Routine

Certain patterns show up again and again.

Using credit to support lifestyle instead of stability.

Ignoring balances because minimum payments feel manageable.

Stacking multiple debts without a clear plan.

Avoiding statements because they create anxiety.

None of these mistakes cause an immediate fall. The routine keeps moving. But timing slips. Flexibility disappears. Small issues compound until one unexpected expense or missed paycheck causes everything to feel overwhelming.

Avoidance is often the real problem.

When you stop looking, you stop correcting. And when corrections stop, small mistakes turn into structural ones.

How Debt Affects More Than Just Money

Debt does not only affect finances. It affects decisions.

When debt is high, options shrink. You stay in jobs you dislike because you need the paycheck. You delay opportunities because you cannot absorb risk. You feel pressure to perform constantly because there is no margin for error.

In cheer terms, this is performing without safety.

Every skill feels heavier. Confidence drops. You are not focused on execution. You are focused on not failing. That mindset increases mistakes and stress.

Controlled debt creates space. It allows you to breathe, adjust, and recover when something does not go perfectly. That space is what allows progress.

Coach's Perspective on Credit and Discipline

A coach would be direct.

Fix timing early.

Do not ignore small mistakes.

Clean reps matter.

Discipline prevents crashes.

No coach waits for a full fall before correcting a routine. Timing is addressed as soon as it drifts. Small corrections early prevent injuries and rebuild confidence.

Credit works the same way. Making payments on time, keeping balances reasonable, and using credit intentionally are the financial version of clean reps. You do not need dramatic moves. You need consistent ones.

Credit rewards consistency, not avoidance.

Game Situations and Decision Points

This is where habits show up.

You carry a balance. Do you create a plan or ignore it?

You qualify for new credit. Do you ask if you should use it or only if you can?

You miss a payment. Do you fix it immediately or let it slide?

You feel stressed about debt. Do you face it or avoid the statements?

Each decision affects timing. One choice rarely defines everything. Repeated choices do.

Missed counts compound. The sooner timing is corrected, the easier the fix. Waiting increases effort and stress.

Common Athlete Mistakes and Their Financial Parallels

Athletes rush timing under pressure.

Financially, that leads to late payments and reactive decisions.

Athletes ignore small errors because nothing crashed.

Financially, that leads to growing balances and rising interest.

Athletes push difficulty too soon.

Financially, that leads to high interest debt and limited flexibility.

The pattern is consistent. Skipped fundamentals always show up later.

Rebuilding Timing After Mistakes

Mistakes will happen. That is normal.

In cheer, mistakes are corrected through walkthroughs, slow reps, and rebuilding confidence. You do not quit the season because of one fall. You clean the routine and move forward.

Financially, the process is similar.

You review balances.

You prioritize payments.

You reduce interest where possible.

You simplify and regain control.

Progress does not require perfection. It requires direction.

Winning the Long Game

Credit and debt do not need to be scary.

They need to be managed.

Clean timing. Consistent payments. Intentional use. When debt is controlled, the routine stays stable. Confidence stays high. Decisions feel proactive instead of reactive.

You stop compensating for past mistakes and start building forward momentum.

Athlete Takeaways

Credit scores reflect consistency, not worth.

Interest is the cost of bad timing.

Not all debt is equal.

Small mistakes grow when ignored.

Clean counts keep the routine together.

When timing is clean, the routine holds. When debt is managed, life feels lighter.

Chapter 5: The Equipment Room of Money: Banking Basics

Every cheer program has an equipment room.

It is not glamorous. No one cheers for it. There are no trophies hanging on the walls and no music playing when someone unlocks the door. But without it, nothing works. Mats, shoes, uniforms, braces, tape, resistance bands, first-aid supplies. Every practice, every stunt, every routine depends on that room being organized, stocked, and reliable.

When equipment is ready and in its place, practice runs smoothly. Athletes focus on performance, not logistics. When equipment is disorganized or neglected, problems show up fast. Practice time gets wasted. Safety risks increase. Frustration builds over things that should have been simple.

Banking plays the same role in your financial life.

It is not exciting. It does not feel like progress. But it is the system that holds everything together. When banking works quietly in the background, you barely notice it. When it fails, stress shows up immediately. Bills bounce. Cards decline. Fees appear. Small issues quickly become distractions that pull energy away from bigger goals.

A strong financial routine depends on a clean banking system.

Checking vs Savings Accounts

Checking accounts are for movement.

They handle deposits, bills, debit card spending, and day-to-day transactions. Money flows in and out constantly. This is where activity happens. Because of that, checking accounts need to be easy to access and easy to monitor.

Savings accounts are for protection and separation.

They hold money you do not want to touch casually. Emergency funds, short-term goals, and buffers live here. The purpose of savings is not convenience. It is distance. That separation creates intention and reduces mistakes.

In cheer terms, checking is the practice mat.

You are on it constantly. It takes wear and tear. It supports daily work.

Savings is the safety mat.

You hope you never need it, but when something goes wrong, it prevents serious damage. You do not casually practice on the safety mat. You respect it.

Keeping checking and savings separate matters more than most people realize. When everything sits in one place, it becomes too easy to overspend, misjudge balances, or dip into money that had a specific purpose. Separation creates clarity.

Why One Account Is Usually Not Enough

Many people start with one account and never move past it.

All income goes in. All expenses go out. Savings, if it happens at all, is whatever is left over. This approach feels simple, but it creates constant confusion. You never quite know how much is safe to spend and how much should be protected.

Athletes understand this instinctively.

You would never store uniforms, practice mats, medical supplies, and competition shoes in one pile and hope it works out. Separation creates order.

Financially, even a basic setup improves stability.

A primary checking account for bills and spending.

A savings account for emergencies.

Possibly a second savings account for short-term goals.

This is not about complexity. It is about organization.

Online Banks vs Traditional Banks

Traditional banks offer physical locations and in-person service. Online banks often offer higher interest rates, fewer fees, and cleaner digital tools. Neither option is automatically better.

In cheer terms, this is choosing equipment brands.

Some teams need access to a local supplier. Others prioritize lightweight gear or durability. The right choice is the one that fits your needs, not the one everyone else uses.

What matters most in banking is reliability.

Can you access your money when you need it?

Are fees transparent and reasonable?

Is customer support available when something goes wrong?

Does the technology make tracking easy or frustrating?

Some people benefit from having both. A traditional bank for in-person needs and an online bank for higher-interest savings. The goal is not loyalty to a brand. The goal is a system that works.

How Money Moves Electronically

Direct deposit, automatic transfers, bill pay, and payment apps move money quickly. Sometimes instantly. Convenience is powerful, but it also hides spending if you are not paying attention.

In cheer terms, this is fast transitions.

When transitions are slow, mistakes are obvious. When everything moves fast, small errors are harder to catch. Money can leave your account before you even realize it happened.

Understanding how and when money moves matters.

When does your paycheck hit?

When do bills actually clear, not just post?

How long do transfers take between accounts?

Which payments are automatic and which are manual?

Many overdrafts and missed payments happen not because someone is irresponsible, but because timing is misunderstood. Money looks available, then disappears when pending transactions clear.

Clarity around timing reduces stress.

Automatic Payments and Their Tradeoffs

Automation can be powerful.

Automatic bill pay prevents missed payments. Automatic transfers build savings without relying on motivation. These systems work best when paired with regular reviews.

Automation without awareness creates blind spots.

Subscriptions renew quietly. Fees go unnoticed. Spending patterns drift. Just because something is automatic does not mean it should be ignored.

In cheer terms, this is setting choreography and never watching the routine again.

You still do walkthroughs. You still clean timing. Automation works when it is paired with attention.

Protecting Yourself From Fraud

Fraud does not usually happen because someone is careless once. It happens when systems are ignored over time.

Weak passwords.

Reused logins.

Unchecked accounts.

Overreliance on debit cards.

Debit cards pull directly from checking accounts. When fraud happens, money is gone immediately. Credit cards add a layer of protection because disputed charges do not remove cash instantly.

In cheer terms, this is safety awareness.

You spot before someone falls. You tape ankles before injury happens. You do not wait for a crash to start caring about safety.

Financial safety works the same way.

Strong passwords.

Account alerts.

Limited debit card use.

Regular statement reviews.

These are not signs of paranoia. They are signs of preparation.

Overdrafts Are Timing Problems

Overdrafts are rarely about irresponsibility.

They happen when timing is off. A bill clears earlier than expected. A deposit hits later than planned. Multiple transactions post at once.

In cheer terms, this is a timing error, not a lack of skill.

Buffers prevent problems. Keeping a small cushion in checking accounts absorbs timing issues. Alerts warn you before balances get too low. Reviewing accounts weekly keeps small issues from growing.

Overdraft fees are preventable with systems, not shame.

Coach's Perspective on Banking Systems

A coach would say it plainly.

Take care of your equipment.

Check it regularly.

Do not ignore warning signs.

Protection prevents problems.

No coach waits until mats tear or shoes fall apart to act. Maintenance is part of performance.

Banking is not exciting, but it is essential. When it works, you get to focus on goals. When it fails, it steals attention from everything else.

Game Situations and Decision Points

This is where organization shows up.

You have multiple accounts. Are they intentional or chaotic?

You rely on convenience. Do you still check balances?

You see a charge you do not recognize. Do you act quickly or wait?

You notice fees. Do you adjust or ignore them?

Small actions protect the system. Small neglect creates friction.

Common Athlete Mistakes and Financial Parallels

Athletes ignore equipment until it fails.

Financially, that leads to overdrafts and fees.

Athletes rush transitions.

Financially, that leads to timing errors and missed payments.

Athletes skip safety checks.

Financially, that leads to fraud and unnecessary loss.

The pattern is consistent. Systems matter more than motivation.

Building a Banking System That Supports Growth

A strong banking setup does not require sophistication.

It requires clarity.

You know which account does what.

You know when money moves.

You know how much buffer exists.

You know where to look when something feels off.

This clarity reduces anxiety. Decisions become easier. Everything else in your financial life becomes easier to manage when the foundation is solid.

Winning the Long Game

Strong routines rely on reliable equipment.

Strong financial lives rely on organized banking.

When your banking system is clean, money flows with less friction. Mistakes are caught early. Stress decreases. You spend less time reacting and more time planning.

Athlete Takeaways

Checking and savings serve different purposes.

One account is rarely enough for clarity.

Choose banks based on fit, not hype.

Fast money movement requires attention.

Protection prevents costly mistakes.

A clean equipment room supports every routine. A clean banking system supports every financial decision that follows.

Part II: Safety, Protection, and Longevity

S*afety first on the mat and with money.*

Cheerleading never skips safety.

Before difficulty increases, athletes learn spotting, proper technique, and how to protect themselves and their teammates. No matter how strong or talented a squad is, safety always comes first. Longevity depends on it.

Money works the same way.

You can budget, save, and invest perfectly, but one unprotected event can undo years of progress. Accidents, illness, liability, and unexpected setbacks do not care how disciplined you are. Protection is what keeps you in the routine when something goes wrong.

This section focuses on awareness and preparation.

Understanding risk.

Knowing what can go wrong.

Putting safeguards in place before they are needed.

Protection is not pessimism. It is professionalism.

Just like cheer, safety does not mean fear. It means confidence. When you know you are protected, you perform better. You take appropriate risks. You stay composed under pressure.

Longevity matters more than short-term performance.

This part of the book shows you how to protect what you are building so you can stay in the game for the long run.

Chapter 6: Risk Awareness and Smart Decision Making

Every cheerleader learns this early.

Not every skill is thrown at full difficulty every time. You earn difficulty through preparation, timing, and trust. A routine that survives season after season is not built on reckless confidence. It is built on knowing when to push and when to stay clean. Athletes who last understand that discipline is not about fear. It is about respect for the process, the team, and the consequences of getting it wrong.

Money decisions work the same way.

Risk is always present. There is no such thing as a risk-free financial life. The difference between smart decisions and costly mistakes is not avoiding risk entirely. It is understanding which risks are worth taking, when they are appropriate, and how much margin for error you actually have.

Just like cheer, problems usually arise when difficulty is rushed before the foundation is ready.

Emotional Risk vs Financial Risk

One of the most important distinctions to learn is the difference between emotional risk and financial risk.

Emotional risk feels urgent.

It shows up as excitement, fear, pressure, confidence, comparison, or anxiety. Emotional risk pushes you to act quickly. It convinces you that waiting means missing out or falling behind. It often sounds like, "Everyone else is doing this," or "I'll figure it out later," or "I feel ready."

Financial risk is measurable.

It considers time, probability, and impact. It asks harder questions. What happens if things do not go as planned? How much downside exists? Can you recover if the decision goes wrong? What does this choice limit or enable in the future?

In cheer terms, emotional risk is throwing a skill because you feel ready in the moment. Financial risk is throwing that same skill because you have trained for it, spotted it, drilled it, and understand exactly what happens if it does not hit.

Learning to separate emotion from measurement is critical.

Emotion is not bad. Confidence is not bad. But emotion without structure leads to rushed difficulty. Measurement without emotion leads to paralysis. Smart decisions balance both.

Why Athletes Are Especially Vulnerable to Emotional Risk

Athletes are trained to trust themselves.

You are taught to push through discomfort. To believe in your preparation. To perform under pressure. These are strengths, but in financial situations, they can backfire if emotion goes unchecked.

Money decisions often come wrapped in identity.

Status. Independence. Success. Comparison. Fear of being behind. Fear of missing an opportunity. These pressures trigger the same competitive instincts that help athletes succeed in sport. Without a framework, those instincts can drive risky financial behavior.

This is not a flaw. It is a mismatch between training and context.

Athletes are used to immediate feedback. Money rarely provides that. Emotional risk fills the gap.

Time Horizon and Flexibility

Risk changes with time.

A decision that is risky in the short term may be reasonable over the long term. A decision that feels safe today may be dangerous if flexibility is limited. Time horizon is one of the most overlooked factors in money decisions.

If you need money soon, risk must be lower. There is no time to recover from mistakes. If time is on your side, you can tolerate more variation because recovery is possible.

Flexibility matters just as much.

Do you have stable income? Do you have savings? Do you have the ability to adjust if things go wrong? Risk is not just about the decision itself. It is about what happens next if the outcome is unfavorable.

In cheer terms, this is routine construction.

Early counts are clean and controlled. You establish rhythm. You build trust. Difficulty comes later, once timing is solid and confidence is earned. You do not open a routine with the riskiest skill and hope it works out.

Time horizon determines how aggressive or conservative decisions should be. Ignoring it leads to rushed difficulty and forced compensations later.

Risk Affects Every Money Decision, Not Just Investing

Many people think risk only applies to investing.

That is a mistake.

Risk shows up in spending choices. In taking on debt. In career decisions. In lifestyle upgrades. In committing to fixed expenses. In relying on uncertain income.

Every financial decision has tradeoffs.

Spending more today reduces flexibility tomorrow.

Taking on debt limits future options.

Skipping savings increases vulnerability.

Changing careers carries income risk.

Ignoring risk does not remove it. It just hides it until pressure increases.

In cheer terms, ignoring risk is skipping safety training.

The routine may look fine until something goes wrong. When it does, the consequences are bigger and recovery is harder.

Awareness allows adjustment. Blindness creates surprise.

Knowing When to Push Difficulty and When to Stay Clean

This is the heart of smart decision making.

There are moments when pushing difficulty makes sense.

Long-term opportunities.

Calculated growth decisions.

Investments aligned with time and flexibility.

Career moves with backup plans.

There are also moments when staying clean matters more.

When stability is fragile.

When income is uncertain.

When debt is high.

When mistakes would be costly.

In cheer, clean execution often wins over risky difficulty. Judges reward consistency. Teams that hit cleanly outperform teams that gamble and miss.

Financially, the same principle applies.

You do not win by taking the biggest risks. You win by taking the right ones at the right time.

Why "Feeling Ready" Is Not the Same as Being Ready

One of the most dangerous signals in money decisions is "I feel ready."

Feeling ready often means emotions are driving the decision. Confidence, excitement, or relief can mask unaddressed risk. Being ready means the numbers support the move. It means contingencies exist. It means the downside is understood and acceptable.

In cheer, feeling ready without preparation leads to falls.

Financially, it leads to regret.

Preparation turns confidence into control.

Coach's Perspective on Risk

A coach would be clear and unapologetic.

Do not rush difficulty.

Earn it.

Protect the routine.

Smart choices win championships.

No good coach encourages athletes to gamble with safety for the sake of excitement. Difficulty is earned through consistency, not bravado.

Risk should be intentional, not accidental.

Intentional risk has boundaries. It has preparation. It has recovery plans. Accidental risk comes from emotion, pressure, or avoidance.

Game Situations and Decision Points

Risk shows up in real moments, not theory.

You feel pressure to act. Do you pause or rush?

An opportunity appears. Do you assess timing and impact?

You are unsure. Do you ask questions or avoid the decision?

You see others succeeding. Do you compare or evaluate your own position?

These moments define outcomes.

Rushing rarely improves results. Pausing rarely closes doors permanently. The ability to slow down under pressure is a competitive advantage.

Common Athlete Mistakes and Their Financial Parallels

Athletes chase difficulty too early.

Financially, that leads to unnecessary risk and forced recovery.

Athletes ignore preparation because confidence feels high.

Financially, that leads to decisions made without understanding consequences.

Athletes trust emotion over process.

Financially, that leads to regret and instability.

The pattern is consistent. When fundamentals are skipped, risk increases and outcomes suffer.

Rebuilding After Risky Decisions

Mistakes will happen.

In cheer, a fall does not end the season. You slow down. You clean the skill. You rebuild trust. You adjust the routine if needed.

Financially, recovery works the same way.

You reassess.

You reduce exposure.

You rebuild buffers.

You regain flexibility.

The goal is not to avoid all risk forever. It is to learn from missteps and move forward smarter.

Winning the Long Game

Smart decisions balance confidence and caution.

When you understand risk, you stop guessing. You stop reacting. You stop chasing outcomes based on emotion. You move intentionally. You protect what you have while building what comes next.

You earn difficulty instead of forcing it.

Just like cheer, long-term success comes from discipline, timing, and trust in the process.

Athlete Takeaways

Emotional risk feels urgent. Financial risk must be measured.

Time horizon changes what level of risk is acceptable.

Every money decision involves tradeoffs, not just investing.

Clean execution often beats risky moves.

Difficulty should be earned, not rushed.

Protect the routine. Build deliberately. Confidence grows when risk is intentional and preparation leads the way.

Chapter 7: Insurance Fundamentals Every Cheerleader Needs

In cheer, safety is not optional.

Before any stunt is thrown, athletes learn proper technique, spotting, and how to protect themselves and their teammates. You drill progressions. You practice falls. You rehearse what to do when something goes wrong. No one walks into a gym hoping to fall, but everyone understands that preparation matters because risk exists. That preparation is what keeps mistakes from turning into serious injuries and short careers.

Insurance serves the same purpose in your financial life.

It is not designed to create wins. It does not make you richer or more successful on its own. Insurance exists to prevent losses from becoming permanent setbacks. It protects the progress you have already worked hard to build so that one bad moment does not undo years of effort.

Just like in cheer, ignoring safety does not make risk disappear. It only makes the consequences worse when something goes wrong.

Why Insurance Feels Unnecessary Until It Is Not

Insurance is easy to dismiss because most days nothing happens.

You feel healthy. Your car starts. Your apartment is fine. Life moves forward normally. When everything is working, insurance feels like an expense without a payoff. Athletes recognize this mindset immediately. Safety drills feel boring until the moment they matter.

The problem is that risk does not announce itself in advance.

Injuries happen in practice, not just competitions. Accidents happen on short drives, not just long trips. Fires, theft, and storms do not wait until it is convenient. Insurance is preparation for uncertainty, not a reaction to disaster.

In cheer terms, insurance is what allows you to keep showing up with confidence, knowing that if something goes wrong, it does not end everything.

Health Insurance Basics

Health insurance protects you from the financial impact of illness or injury.

Medical costs can add up quickly, even for routine care. A single emergency room visit, diagnostic test, or procedure can cost thousands of dollars. Without coverage, those costs do not just create stress. They can derail savings, create debt, and limit options for years.

In cheer terms, health insurance is your safety mat.

You do not think about the mat when everything goes right. You trust that it is there. But when something goes wrong, it absorbs the impact and prevents serious damage.

Understanding your health insurance matters.

What services are covered.

What you pay out of pocket.

When deductibles apply.

How networks work.

Many people carry health insurance without truly understanding it. That leads to surprises at the worst times. Knowing your plan is part of preparation, not paranoia.

Athletes study safety rules because knowing what to do reduces panic. Health insurance works the same way. Knowledge replaces fear with control.

Auto and Renters Insurance

Auto insurance protects you when driving.

It covers damage, injuries, and liability when accidents happen. Even careful drivers cannot control other people on the road. Driving without proper coverage exposes you to financial risk that can follow you for years.

Renters insurance protects your belongings and provides liability coverage.

Many people skip renters insurance because they believe they do not own much. This is almost always a mistake. Theft, fire, and water damage can destroy everything you own in a single event. Liability coverage also matters. If someone is injured in your apartment, renters insurance can protect you from legal and financial consequences.

In cheer terms, this is personal safety equipment.

You do not skip braces, tape, or proper shoes because you feel fine that day. You wear them because risk exists even when you feel confident. Renters insurance is inexpensive relative to the protection it provides, yet it is one of the most commonly skipped coverages.

Skipping protection does not save money in the long run. It shifts risk onto you.

Homeowners Insurance

Homeowners insurance protects both your property and your liability.

It covers damage to your home, belongings, and certain risks involving others. It also provides protection if someone is injured on your property. Owning a home without proper insurance is like throwing advanced stunts without spotters. The risk is not theoretical. It is real and costly.

Coverage needs change over time.

As home values increase, as belongings accumulate, and as life circumstances change, insurance should be reviewed. Many people set a policy once and never look at it again. That creates gaps between what they think is covered and what actually is.

In cheer terms, routines evolve.

You do not perform the same routine year after year without adjustments. Insurance should evolve with your life in the same way.

Deductibles, Premiums, and Coverage Limits

Insurance has three core components.

Premiums are what you pay regularly.

Deductibles are what you pay when something happens.

Coverage limits are the maximum the policy will pay.

Balancing these is about understanding risk tolerance and cash flow.

Lower premiums often come with higher deductibles. Higher coverage limits often cost more. There is no universal best choice. The right balance depends on your financial position, savings, and ability to absorb short term costs.

In cheer terms, this is choosing appropriate difficulty.

Too little protection increases risk and exposure. Too much protection can strain resources unnecessarily. The goal is not maximum coverage at any cost. The goal is coverage that fits your routine and your ability to recover if something happens.

Choosing insurance blindly is like choosing difficulty without considering conditioning. Thoughtful decisions protect performance.

Why Insurance Is Not About Fear

Many people avoid insurance conversations because they feel negative.

Thinking about accidents, illness, or loss is uncomfortable. Athletes understand this tension. No one enjoys practicing falls or emergency procedures. But preparation does not mean expecting failure. It means respecting reality.

Insurance is not pessimism.

It is confidence backed by preparation.

It allows you to take appropriate risks elsewhere because you know the downside is limited. Without insurance, every unexpected event becomes a threat to your entire routine.

Coach's Perspective on Safety and Longevity

A coach would emphasize safety without apology.

Protect yourself.

Do not cut corners.

Prepare for what you cannot predict.

Longevity matters more than short-term excitement.

No coach sacrifices athlete safety for momentary success. The goal is to keep athletes healthy, confident, and able to perform over time.

Insurance plays the same role financially.

It keeps you in the game. It allows recovery. It protects progress. It gives you the ability to move forward after setbacks instead of starting over.

Game Situations and Decision Points

This is where insurance decisions become real.

You feel healthy. Do you still prioritize coverage?

You want lower premiums. Do you understand the tradeoffs?

Life changes. New job, new car, new home. Do you review protection?

You have not looked at policies in years. Do you assume they still fit?

Ignoring insurance does not remove risk. It only increases exposure.

Small decisions made today determine whether future setbacks are manageable or overwhelming.

Common Athlete Mistakes and Financial Parallels

Athletes skip safety steps because nothing has gone wrong yet.

Financially, that leads to exposure when something eventually does.

Athletes underestimate risk because confidence is high.

Financially, that leads to costly surprises.

Athletes avoid boring preparation.

Financially, that leads to setbacks that could have been prevented.

The pattern is consistent. Safety ignored early becomes regret later.

How Insurance Supports Confidence and Growth

When insurance is handled correctly, it fades into the background.

You stop worrying about worst-case scenarios because you know they are covered. That mental freedom matters. It allows focus on goals, performance, and growth instead of constant anxiety.

In cheer terms, this is trusting your spotters.

You perform better when you know protection is in place. You move with confidence instead of hesitation.

Insurance does not eliminate risk. It manages it.

Winning the Long Game

Insurance allows you to take appropriate risks without fear.

It protects the progress you have worked hard to build. It prevents one bad moment from defining your future. It supports stability so growth can happen.

Safety is not weakness.

It is strategy.

Athletes who last understand this. Financially, the same principle applies. Preparation creates resilience. Protection creates confidence. Longevity beats short-term shortcuts every time.

Athlete Takeaways

Insurance protects against major setbacks, not daily inconveniences.

Health insurance acts as your safety mat.

Auto, renters, and homeowners coverage protect against real-world risk.

Deductibles, premiums, and limits must be balanced intentionally.

Coverage should evolve as your life changes.

Safety keeps you in the routine. Preparation keeps you progressing. Insurance ensures that when life hits unexpectedly, you are still standing, ready to keep going.

Chapter 8: Life, Disability, and Liability Protection

In cheer, you do not just protect the stunt.

You protect the athlete.

Spotters are trained. Bases communicate. Coaches plan for what happens if timing slips or a grip fails. Safety plans exist because the real risk is not the fall itself. The real risk is what happens after a fall if no one was prepared to absorb the impact, stabilize the athlete, and prevent a bad moment from becoming a long-term injury.

Life, disability, and liability insurance serve the same role in your financial life.

They are not about today's routine. They are not about what is going well right now. They exist to protect your future when something unexpected happens. They protect people, income, and progress when the routine cannot continue as planned.

Just like in cheer, hoping nothing goes wrong is not a strategy. Preparation is.

Why Protection Beyond Basics Matters

Earlier protections like health, auto, renters, and homeowners insurance focus on immediate risks. Medical bills. Property damage. Accidents. Those are essential, but they are not the whole picture.

Life, disability, and liability coverage address deeper risks:

- What happens if income stops
- What happens if someone depends on you financially
- What happens if a single event puts everything you have built at risk

These coverages are less visible day to day, which is why they are often delayed or avoided. Athletes understand this pattern well. The most important safety systems are usually the least exciting ones.

Term vs Permanent Life Insurance

Life insurance exists to protect the people who depend on you.

If someone relies on your income, your presence, or your financial support, life insurance is not optional. It is not about you. It is about the impact your absence would have on others.

Term Life Insurance

Term life insurance provides coverage for a specific period of time. Ten years. Twenty years. Thirty years. It is designed to cover the years when financial risk is highest.

Common uses include:

- Replacing income for a spouse or partner
- Supporting children while they are dependent
- Paying off a mortgage or other debts
- Covering education or living expenses

Term insurance is typically straightforward and affordable. You choose the coverage amount and the term length, and if something happens during that period, the benefit is paid.

In cheer terms, term insurance is your basic safety setup.

It is clean. It is effective. It does exactly what it is supposed to do. Most people who need life insurance need term insurance first. There is no benefit to complexity if the core protection is missing.

Permanent Life Insurance

Permanent life insurance lasts for your entire life and includes additional features beyond basic protection. It is more complex, more expensive, and not appropriate for everyone.

Permanent insurance can make sense in specific situations:

- Long-term estate planning needs
- Certain business planning scenarios
- Situations where lifelong coverage is necessary

In cheer terms, permanent insurance is advanced equipment.

Advanced equipment is not bad, but it is not where you start. You do not add complexity unless it fits your routine, your role, and your long-term plan. Using advanced equipment without understanding it increases risk rather than reducing it.

The goal with life insurance is protection, not sophistication.

Disability Insurance and Income Protection

Your ability to earn income is often your most valuable asset.

This is especially true early and mid-career, when savings are limited and future earning power is high. If income stops due to illness or injury, everything else is affected. Savings disappear. Bills continue. Long-term plans stall.

Disability insurance protects that income.

Many people assume disability insurance is unnecessary because they feel healthy or believe serious injury will not happen to them. That assumption is dangerous. Disabilities are far more common than people realize, and many are caused by illness rather than accidents.

In cheer terms, disability insurance protects the athlete, not just the routine.

If the athlete cannot perform, the routine stops entirely. It does not matter how well designed the routine is. Without the athlete, nothing moves forward.

Short-Term vs Long-Term Disability

Short-term disability typically covers a portion of income for a limited period, such as a few months. Long-term disability can last for years or even until retirement age, depending on the policy.

Both serve a purpose.

Short-term coverage helps with temporary disruptions. Long-term coverage protects against life-altering events. Gaps between the two can create serious financial stress if not planned for.

Disability insurance is often overlooked because it is uncomfortable to think about. But discomfort is not a reason to leave exposure unaddressed.

Umbrella Liability Coverage

Umbrella insurance provides additional liability protection beyond basic policies like auto and homeowners insurance.

It covers situations where claims, lawsuits, or damages exceed standard coverage limits. These events are uncommon, but when they happen, the impact can be severe.

Lawsuits do not only target the reckless. They often target whoever appears to have assets or income. As your life grows, your exposure grows with it.

In cheer terms, umbrella coverage is having extra spotters when difficulty increases.

You may never need them. You hope you never need them. But when difficulty increases, you do not rely on the minimum level of protection. You build in margin.

Umbrella insurance protects:

- Savings
- Investments
- Property
- Future income

It protects everything you are building from being undone by a single event.

Common Insurance Mistakes Athletes Make

Certain patterns show up repeatedly.

- Assuming nothing bad will happen because nothing has happened yet
- Skipping coverage because it feels unnecessary or boring
- Buying insurance without understanding what it actually covers
- Overcomplicating decisions and getting stuck
- Avoiding decisions entirely because the topic feels uncomfortable

These mistakes are not about intelligence.

They are about unfamiliar systems and emotional avoidance. Athletes are trained to face physical discomfort, not administrative complexity. Insurance feels abstract, so it gets postponed.

Preparation reduces fear.

Once coverage is understood and in place, anxiety drops. Decisions become clearer. Confidence increases.

Why Avoidance Is the Real Risk

Many people believe that delaying insurance decisions keeps them safe from making a mistake. In reality, avoidance increases exposure.

Risk does not pause because you are uncomfortable. It continues quietly in the background.

In cheer, ignoring safety procedures does not reduce risk. It increases it. Financial protection works the same way.

Coach's Perspective on Protecting the Athlete

A coach would not sugarcoat this.

Protect yourself.

Plan for setbacks.

Do not leave your future exposed.

Smart protection is part of discipline.

No responsible coach sacrifices athlete safety for convenience or optimism. Protection is not pessimism. It is respect for reality.

Insurance decisions are not about fear. They are about responsibility to yourself and to others who rely on you.

Game Situations and Decision Points

These decisions show up at key moments.

You feel healthy. Do you still protect income?

You have dependents. Do you plan now or postpone?

Your income grows. Do you update protection?

Your assets increase. Do you add liability coverage?

Every delay is a choice, even if it does not feel like one.

Avoidance does not equal safety. It just leaves risk unmanaged.

Common Athlete Mistakes and Financial Parallels

Athletes underestimate risk when things feel easy.

Financially, that leads to exposure.

Athletes rely on hope instead of preparation.

Financially, that leads to stress when something goes wrong.

Athletes avoid uncomfortable training.

Financially, that leads to regret when protection was needed.

The patterns are the same. The consequences are just different.

How Protection Enables Confidence and Growth

Proper protection does not limit progress. It enables it.

When life, disability, and liability risks are addressed:

- You take career opportunities with more confidence
- You invest and plan without constant fear
- You recover faster from setbacks
- You protect the people and goals that matter most

In cheer terms, this is trusting your safety system.

When protection is in place, performance improves. Hesitation disappears. Confidence grows.

Winning the Long Game

Life, disability, and liability protection allow you to move forward with confidence.

They turn unknown risks into manageable outcomes. They ensure that one unexpected event does not erase years of effort. They protect not just today's routine, but your future seasons as well.

Strong routines protect the athletes.

Strong financial plans do the same.

Longevity is not accidental. It is built through preparation, discipline, and respect for risk.

Athlete Takeaways

Life insurance protects the people who rely on you.

Disability insurance protects your ability to earn.

Umbrella coverage protects everything you build.

Insurance mistakes come from avoidance, not ignorance.

Protection supports longevity, confidence, and progress.

In cheer, safety allows athletes to perform at their best.
In life, protection allows you to build forward without fear.
Protect the athlete. Protect the future.

Part III: Building Momentum (Investing Fundamentals)

M*omentum is built through clean execution.*

In cheer, momentum does not come from rushing.

It comes from timing, balance, and clean transitions. When the basics are solid, movement flows. When they are not, everything feels forced and unstable.

Investing works the same way.

Momentum in your financial life is not created by big wins or perfect timing. It is built through consistent decisions, patience, and discipline over time. Small actions, repeated correctly, create progress that compounds.

This part of the book introduces investing fundamentals without hype or shortcuts. The focus is on understanding how investing works, how risk and reward interact, and how to stay consistent when emotions run high.

Just like cheer, investing rewards preparation and clean execution. You do not chase momentum. You build it.

These chapters will help you understand how to move forward intentionally, avoid common mistakes, and trust the process as progress builds.

Momentum is not an accident.

It is the result of doing the right things, in the right order, again and again.

Chapter 9: How Financial Markets Really Work

From the outside, financial markets can look chaotic.

Prices move constantly. Headlines change daily. Opinions swing from optimism to panic overnight. Social media amplifies noise. Commentators argue. Numbers flash red and green. For someone who has never been taught how markets actually work, it feels unpredictable and intimidating, like watching a routine with no understanding of counts, scoring, or rules.

But markets are not chaos.

They are systems.

Once you understand how they function, the noise fades. The movement starts to make sense. You stop reacting to every headline and start seeing structure, patterns, and purpose. Just like cheer, what looks confusing from the outside becomes logical once you understand the framework.

Why Markets Feel So Confusing at First

Most people are introduced to markets through outcomes, not explanations.

They hear about gains and losses. Booms and crashes. Someone "made a killing." Someone else "lost everything." Rarely does anyone explain what is actually happening underneath those stories. Without context, movement feels random and emotionally charged.

Athletes experience something similar when watching elite competition without training.

From the stands, routines look fast and overwhelming. Once you know counts, timing, and scoring, you see control instead of chaos. Markets work the same way.

Confusion comes from lack of structure, not lack of intelligence.

How Markets Actually Function

At their core, markets exist to exchange ownership and capital.

Companies need money to grow. To build products, hire people, expand operations, or innovate. Investors provide that money in exchange for ownership or repayment. Markets are the mechanism that connects those two sides.

Prices move because expectations change.

Markets are not reacting only to what happened today. They are constantly adjusting based on what participants believe will happen in the future. Earnings projections, interest rates, innovation, competition, and economic conditions all influence expectations.

In cheer terms, this is competition scoring.

Judges are not reacting to one motion or one count. They are evaluating the entire routine. Difficulty, execution, timing, deductions, and overall performance all matter. A small wobble does not ruin everything if the routine is strong overall. Markets think the same way.

They are forward-looking systems, not emotional scorecards.

Stocks, Bonds, and What Ownership Really Means

One of the biggest misunderstandings about markets is not knowing what you actually own.

When you buy a stock, you are buying ownership in a company.

That ownership connects your outcome to the long-term success of the business. If the company grows, becomes more profitable, and creates value over time, owners benefit. If it struggles, owners feel that impact.

Stocks are not lottery tickets. They are claims on future cash flow and business success.

Bonds are different.

When you buy a bond, you are lending money. You are not owning the company. You are acting as a creditor. In return, you receive interest and expect repayment of principal.

In cheer terms, stocks are being part of the routine.

Your performance is tied to execution. You are on the mat. You feel the highs and lows.

Bonds are like supporting from the sidelines.

You provide stability. You do not participate in the stunts, but you play a role in keeping the program funded and steady.

Both have value. Both serve different purposes. Confusion comes when people expect one to behave like the other.

Why Balance Matters More Than Picking Winners

Many new investors believe success comes from picking the right stock or timing the market perfectly.

This belief mirrors a common cheer mistake.

Teams that chase the hardest skill instead of building a balanced routine often struggle. Difficulty alone does not win. Execution, timing, and consistency matter more.

Markets reward balance.

Different assets behave differently under different conditions. Some provide growth. Some provide stability. Some reduce volatility. A well-structured approach acknowledges that no single asset performs best all the time.

Balance is not about being conservative. It is about being intentional.

Market Cycles and Why Volatility Is Normal

Markets move in cycles.

Growth. Slowdown. Decline. Recovery. Expansion again.

This pattern repeats over decades. The timing and triggers change, but the cycle itself is constant. Volatility is not a flaw in the system. It is part of how markets function.

In cheer terms, this is season flow.

Some practices feel clean and confident. Others feel messy. Some weeks progress is obvious. Other weeks feel like regression. That does not mean training is broken. It means improvement is not linear.

Volatility becomes dangerous only when emotion replaces discipline.

The biggest mistakes in markets usually come from reacting to normal movement as if it is an emergency. Selling because of fear. Buying because of hype. Abandoning plans mid-cycle.

Athletes know this instinct well. Panic creates mistakes. Calm execution preserves control.

Short-Term Noise vs Long-Term Outcomes

Markets generate constant information.

Prices update every second. News breaks daily. Opinions flood timelines. This creates the illusion that action is always required.

But most of that information is noise.

Long-term outcomes are driven by fundamentals. Business growth. Innovation. Productivity. Economic expansion. These forces move slowly compared to headlines.

In cheer terms, this is focusing on the routine, not the crowd.

Crowd reactions change moment to moment. Judges score the routine as a whole. Athletes who look to the crowd mid-performance lose timing. Investors who focus on daily noise lose discipline.

Understanding this distinction reduces anxiety dramatically.

Long-Term Strategy vs Chasing Hype

Chasing hype is one of the most common market mistakes.

Hot tips. Viral trends. Fear-based selling. Excitement-driven buying. These behaviors feel justified in the moment because they are emotionally charged and socially reinforced.

In cheer terms, this is changing choreography mid-performance.

It feels responsive, but it destroys timing. It pulls you off counts. It creates confusion and inconsistency.

Long-term strategies are built before emotion enters the picture.

They account for risk tolerance. Time horizon. Goals. They expect volatility and plan for it instead of reacting to it.

Clean execution beats risky improvisation.

Momentum is built by staying on counts, not by reacting to every signal.

Why Patience Is a Competitive Advantage

Markets do not reward impatience.

They reward:

- Time
- Consistency
- Discipline
- Understanding

This is frustrating for people who are used to immediate feedback.

Athletes are accustomed to seeing improvement quickly when effort is applied. Markets do not work that way. Progress is often invisible for long stretches, then obvious in hindsight.

Patience is not passive.

It is active discipline. It is choosing not to react when reaction feels tempting. It is trusting preparation and process.

In cheer, routines are won before competition day. Markets work the same way.

Coach's Perspective on Markets

A coach would be blunt.

Ignore the crowd.

Trust the routine.

Stick to the plan.

Consistency wins.

No coach allows athletes to change routines based on audience reaction. No coach encourages panic mid-performance. The expectation is trust in preparation.

Markets reward the same mindset.

Game Situations and Decision Points

Understanding markets matters most in real moments.

Prices drop. Do you panic or stay disciplined?

A trend explodes. Do you chase or evaluate?

Headlines sound alarming. Do you react or revisit fundamentals?

You feel uncertain. Do you abandon the plan or refine it?

These moments define outcomes far more than market movement itself.

Your response matters more than what the market does next.

Common Athlete Mistakes and Financial Parallels

Athletes react emotionally under pressure.

Financially, that leads to poor timing.

Athletes change routines too often.

Financially, that leads to inconsistency and underperformance.

Athletes chase attention instead of execution.

Financially, that leads to hype-driven decisions.

The parallels are direct. The consequences compound over time.

Reframing Market Movement as Information, Not Threat

Once you understand market structure, movement becomes information.

Price changes reflect updated expectations. Volatility reflects uncertainty. Cycles reflect economic rhythms. None of these require panic.

In cheer terms, this is reading judges' feedback.

Feedback is not an attack. It is data. It tells you where to adjust, not whether to quit.

Markets provide constant feedback. The goal is to interpret it calmly, not emotionally.

Winning the Long Game

Markets are not designed to reward impatience or emotion.

They reward understanding, discipline, and long-term commitment. They reward people who respect the system instead of fighting it. Once you see the structure, fear fades and confidence grows.

You stop guessing.

You stop chasing.

You start executing.

Just like cheer, mastery comes from repetition, trust, and staying on counts.

Athlete Takeaways

Markets are systems, not chaos.

Prices reflect expectations about the future.

Stocks represent ownership. Bonds represent lending.

Volatility is normal, not dangerous.

Long-term strategies outperform hype.

Your response matters more than market noise.

Stay on counts. Trust the routine. Let discipline do the work.

Chapter 10: Risk, Return, and the Power of Compounding

In cheer, nothing happens all at once.

Strength is built rep by rep. Flexibility improves slowly. Timing gets cleaner over weeks and months. Even the most impressive routines are the result of thousands of quiet practices that no one ever sees. There is no single workout, stretch, or practice that suddenly creates excellence. Progress comes from repetition, patience, and trust in the process.

The biggest improvements rarely come from one perfect practice. They come from showing up consistently and letting progress stack.

Investing works the same way.

Risk, return, and compounding are not separate ideas. They work together. When you understand how they interact, small and ordinary actions become powerful over time. When you do not understand them, markets feel intimidating, progress feels slow, and mistakes feel personal instead of structural.

This chapter is about slowing things down and seeing the long game clearly.

Risk and Reward Always Travel Together

Every reward comes with risk.

There is no investment that offers high returns with no uncertainty. If someone promises that, they are selling fantasy, not reality. Markets do not work that way. Progress requires exposure to uncertainty. Growth demands participation in outcomes that are not guaranteed.

Higher potential returns usually come with more ups and downs. Lower risk usually means slower progress. That tradeoff never disappears. It exists in every market, in every era, and for every investor.

In cheer terms, this is difficulty selection.

Higher difficulty increases scoring potential, but it also increases the chance of mistakes. Lower difficulty reduces risk, but it caps how far the routine can go. Teams that understand this do not blindly chase the hardest skills. They choose difficulty that fits their timing, conditioning, and confidence.

The goal is not maximum difficulty.

The goal is appropriate difficulty.

In investing, risk should match readiness. That includes both financial readiness and emotional readiness. Taking more risk than you can tolerate leads to panic when volatility shows up. Panic leads to poor decisions. Poor decisions turn temporary discomfort into permanent damage.

Risk is not the enemy. Mismanaged risk is.

Why Risk Is So Often Misunderstood

Many people think risk means danger.

That belief creates fear and avoidance. It causes people to either take too much risk without understanding it or avoid investing entirely because uncertainty feels uncomfortable.

In reality, risk means uncertainty.

It means outcomes are not guaranteed. It means results will vary. It means there will be periods where progress feels slow or even negative. That uncertainty is uncomfortable, especially for people who value control and predictability.

Athletes understand uncertainty intuitively.

In cheer, uncertainty exists every time a routine hits the mat. Even well-trained teams do not know exactly how it will go. Preparation reduces uncertainty, but it never removes it completely. There is always the possibility of a bobble, a timing slip, or a missed grip.

The same is true with investing.

Preparation reduces risk. Diversification reduces risk. Time reduces risk. But none of them eliminate uncertainty entirely.

Risk is not something to eliminate.

It is something to manage.

Volatility vs Permanent Loss

This distinction is critical.

Volatility is movement.

Prices rise and fall. Markets react to news, emotion, and expectations. Volatility feels stressful because numbers change quickly and unpredictably. But volatility is normal. It is part of how markets function.

Permanent loss is different.

Permanent loss happens when money cannot recover. This usually occurs not because markets moved, but because decisions were made at the wrong time. Panic selling during fear. Abandoning a long-term plan after a temporary decline. Concentrating too much in one area and refusing to adjust.

In cheer terms, volatility is a wobble.

Wobbles happen even in strong routines. Judges expect them. Teams recover from them. A wobble does not end the routine.

Permanent loss is a fall.

Falls usually come from breakdowns in preparation, trust, or discipline. They are not caused by the existence of difficulty. They are caused by mismanagement of it.

Learning to tolerate volatility is what prevents permanent loss.

This is one of the most important skills an investor can develop. The ability to sit with discomfort without reacting emotionally is a competitive advantage.

Why Emotional Reactions Cause Real Damage

Most long-term investing damage is self-inflicted.

Markets do not usually destroy long-term plans. People do. Selling during fear locks in losses. Chasing gains during excitement leads to buying at inflated prices. Constantly changing strategies breaks compounding.

In cheer terms, this is panicking after a small mistake.

One rushed correction leads to another. Timing gets worse. Confidence drops. The routine falls apart not because of the initial wobble, but because of the reaction to it.

Discipline is what separates temporary discomfort from permanent damage.

Discipline does not mean ignoring reality. It means responding intentionally instead of emotionally.

Compounding Over Time

Compounding is progress building on progress.

Returns earn returns. Growth stacks on top of growth. Small gains accumulate. Time magnifies consistency. Compounding is not a trick or a shortcut. It is the natural result of staying invested and allowing growth to layer.

Compounding is not exciting at first.

Early progress feels slow. Results feel insignificant. It can feel like nothing is happening. That is normal. Compounding works quietly in the beginning because the base is small.

In cheer terms, compounding is muscle memory.

Early reps feel awkward. Strength feels limited. Timing feels inconsistent. You work hard without seeing dramatic results. Then one day, skills feel easier. Strength shows up without conscious effort. Timing feels automatic.

The work did not suddenly pay off. It paid off gradually until the results became visible.

Compounding works the same way.

Time does the heavy lifting.

Why Compounding Rewards Consistency, Not Intensity

Compounding does not reward intensity.

One big effort does not replace years of steady work. A single great year does not matter as much as decades of consistent participation. Trying to force results quickly often backfires.

In cheer, skipping practice and hoping for a strong competition rarely works. Reps create confidence. Confidence creates execution. Execution creates consistency.

In investing, regular contributions, patience, and staying invested allow compounding to do its work. The habit matters more than the amount at first.

Stopping and starting breaks momentum.

Pulling out and jumping back in resets progress. Each interruption reduces the power of compounding because time is lost.

Consistency keeps the engine running.

The Cost of Waiting

Waiting feels safe.

Many people delay investing because they want more certainty, better timing, or more confidence. They tell themselves they will start later, when things feel clearer or when they have more money.

That delay has a cost.

Time is the one resource you cannot replace. You can earn more money. You can rebuild savings. You cannot rewind years of missed compounding.

In cheer terms, skipping reps slows improvement.

You cannot compress years of practice into a few weeks later. The body needs time. The nervous system needs repetition. Skills need space to develop.

Waiting does not remove risk.

It removes opportunity.

Starting small and staying consistent is more powerful than waiting for perfect conditions.

Why Starting Matters More Than Starting Big

You do not need to start perfectly.

You need to start.

Small contributions build habits. Habits build discipline. Discipline allows compounding to work. The size of the first step matters far less than the fact that it happens.

Many athletes hesitate because they want everything to be perfect. Perfect timing. Perfect form. Perfect readiness. Coaches know better.

In cheer, perfect technique develops through repetition, not hesitation.

Momentum comes from movement. Confidence grows after action, not before it.

Investing works the same way.

How Risk, Compounding, and Time Work Together

These three concepts are inseparable.

Risk creates the possibility of return.

Time allows returns to stack.

Compounding magnifies the result.

Remove one, and progress stalls.

Too much risk without time leads to volatility-driven mistakes.

Time without risk leads to stagnation.

Risk without discipline leads to permanent loss.

Balance creates momentum.

Coach's Perspective on Patience and Execution

A coach would emphasize patience and discipline.

Do not rush difficulty.

Do not freeze under pressure.

Trust the reps.

Let time work with you.

Progress does not come from forcing results. It comes from showing up consistently, cleaning execution, and staying committed through uncomfortable stretches.

Markets reward the same mindset.

Game Situations and Decision Points

This is where theory becomes reality.

Markets dip. Do you stay disciplined or panic?

You feel uncertain. Do you pause thoughtfully or react emotionally?

You tell yourself you will start later. Do you understand what you are giving up?

Returns feel slow. Do you quit or stay consistent?

Time rewards those who participate.

Your response during uncomfortable moments matters far more than your decisions during calm ones.

Common Athlete Mistakes and Financial Parallels

Athletes chase difficulty too quickly.

Financially, that leads to unnecessary risk and emotional reactions.

Athletes avoid discomfort.

Financially, that leads to delay and missed opportunity.

Athletes expect instant results.

Financially, that leads to frustration and abandonment of good plans.

Discipline corrects all three.

Reframing Progress

Progress is rarely dramatic in real time.

It feels boring. Uneventful. Ordinary. That does not mean it is ineffective. It means it is working.

In cheer, the most important practices are often the least exciting ones. The same is true with investing.

Quiet consistency beats loud effort.

Winning the Long Game

Risk is part of growth.

Compounding is how growth becomes meaningful.

Volatility is normal. Panic is optional. Time rewards those who stay disciplined and consistent. When you respect risk, trust compounding, and stay patient, momentum builds naturally.

Just like cheer, success does not come from one perfect moment.

It comes from clean execution over time.

Athlete Takeaways

Risk and reward always travel together.

Risk means uncertainty, not danger.

Volatility is normal. Permanent loss is avoidable.

Compounding rewards consistency, not intensity.

Waiting has a real cost.

Starting small beats waiting for perfect conditions.

Show up. Stay disciplined. Trust the reps.

Over time, progress stacks.

Chapter 11: Stocks Without the Spotlight

In cheer, highlight moments get the attention.

Big skills. High difficulty. Perfect tosses. Those moments make the crowd react. But every experienced athlete knows the truth. A routine is not won by highlights alone. It is won by clean execution, consistency, and fundamentals that hold under pressure.

Stocks are treated the same way.

They get the hype. The headlines. The excitement. They are often framed as fast money, big wins, and overnight success. That framing causes people to misunderstand what stocks actually are and how they are meant to work.

Stocks are not lottery tickets. They are ownership.

What Owning Stock Really Means

When you buy a stock, you are buying ownership in a business.

You are not betting on a ticker symbol. You are purchasing a small piece of a company that produces goods or services, hires people, earns profits, and competes in the marketplace.

That ownership entitles you to participate in the company's success or failure over time.

In cheer terms, owning stock is joining the team. You are now part of the routine. Your outcome depends on preparation, execution, and consistency, not one moment.

Stock prices move daily. Businesses grow over years.

Understanding that difference changes behavior.

Why Price Movement Distracts From Reality

Most people focus on price.

They watch charts. They react to swings. They assume price tells the full story. It does not.

In cheer terms, this is judging a routine by one count instead of the entire performance.

Price reflects emotion in the short term. Ownership reflects value over the long term.

When you remember that you own businesses, not charts, patience becomes easier.

Growth vs Value Investing

Stocks are often categorized as growth or value.

Growth investing focuses on companies expected to grow faster than average. These companies often reinvest profits to expand. They may not look cheap, but investors expect future growth to justify the price.

Value investing focuses on companies that appear undervalued relative to fundamentals. These companies may be mature, temporarily out of favor, or overlooked.

Neither approach is inherently better.

In cheer terms, growth investing is higher difficulty. Value investing is strong fundamentals. Both can succeed. Higher difficulty increases upside and risk. Fundamentals emphasize consistency and durability.

Many investors struggle because they chase one style emotionally instead of understanding the role each can play.

Why Style Chasing Creates Problems

Styles rotate.

Growth leads. Then value leads. Then growth returns. Investors who chase what is working often arrive late and leave early.

In cheer terms, this is switching routines every time another team scores well. Execution breaks down.

Consistency matters more than style.

Dividends and Total Return

Dividends are cash payments companies distribute to shareholders.

Some investors focus heavily on dividends. Others ignore them entirely. Both approaches miss the point.

What matters is total return.

Total return includes price appreciation plus dividends received.

In cheer terms, dividends are steady execution. Price growth is difficulty. You need both over time.

A company does not need to pay dividends to be valuable. A dividend alone does not make an investment good.

Total return reflects the full outcome of ownership.

Why Dividends Feel Comforting

Dividends feel tangible.

You receive cash. You see progress. That can provide psychological comfort, especially during volatile markets.

In cheer terms, this is clean execution providing confidence even when difficulty feels shaky.

Dividends can play a role. They should not drive decisions alone.

Common Stock Investing Myths

Several myths cause investors to make poor decisions.

Myth 1: Stocks Are Too Risky

Stocks are volatile in the short term. Over long periods, they have historically rewarded patience. Risk depends on time horizon and behavior, not just the asset.

In cheer terms, difficulty is risky without training. With preparation, it becomes manageable.

Myth 2: You Have to Pick Winners

Most people believe success requires finding the next big stock. In reality, diversification reduces reliance on being right.

In cheer terms, no routine depends on one athlete doing everything.

Myth 3: Timing Matters More Than Consistency

Waiting for the perfect time leads to inaction. Consistent participation matters more.

In cheer terms, skipping reps because conditions are not perfect delays progress.

Myth 4: Stocks Are Gambling

Gambling relies on odds and luck. Investing relies on ownership, discipline, and time.

In cheer terms, competition is not gambling. It is preparation meeting execution.

Why Emotion Is the Real Risk

The biggest risk in stock investing is not volatility.

It is behavior.

Fear during downturns. Overconfidence during rallies. Comparison when others talk about wins. These emotions push investors to buy high and sell low.

In cheer terms, this is letting nerves dictate timing instead of counts.

Stocks reward discipline. They punish reaction.

How Stocks Fit Into a Balanced Routine

Stocks are designed for growth.

They are meant to power long-term progress, not provide short-term comfort. They work best when paired with stabilizing elements like bonds and cash.

In cheer terms, stocks are difficulty. Difficulty wins only when supported by control and balance.

Stocks should be sized appropriately so volatility does not force bad decisions.

Coach's Perspective

A coach would strip away the hype.

Know what you own.

Trust the fundamentals.

Do not chase highlights.

Execute consistently.

Clean routines beat flashy routines that fall.

Stocks reward preparation, patience, and discipline.

Game Situations and Decision Points

Markets drop. Do you remember you own businesses or react to price?

Stocks rally. Do you chase or stay balanced?

You hear others brag. Do you compare or trust your routine?

Your response matters more than the market.

Common Athlete Mistakes and Financial Parallels

Athletes chase highlights.

Financially, that leads to speculation.

Athletes ignore fundamentals.

Financially, that leads to poor decisions.

Athletes panic under pressure.

Financially, that leads to selling at the wrong time.

Awareness corrects all three.

Winning the Long Game

Stocks are powerful tools when used correctly.

They allow ownership in productive businesses. They harness growth over time. They reward consistency, not brilliance.

Success with stocks is not about hype. It is about execution.

Just like cheer, routines win when fundamentals hold under pressure.

Athlete Takeaways

- Owning stock means owning part of a business
- Growth and value are styles, not guarantees
- Dividends are part of total return, not the whole story
- Stock investing is not gambling when done with discipline
- Emotion is the biggest risk
- Clean execution beats hype

Chapter 12: Bonds and Staying Balanced

In cheer, balance is everything.

A routine does not work if all the energy goes into difficulty without control. Balance keeps stunts stable, landings clean, and transitions smooth. Without it, even strong athletes struggle to stay upright.

Bonds play that same role in investing.

They are not designed to steal the spotlight. They exist to provide balance, stability, and structure when things get shaky. Bonds do not make headlines, but they often determine whether a portfolio holds together under pressure.

Why Bonds Are Often Misunderstood

Many people dismiss bonds as boring.

They do not move like stocks. They do not promise explosive growth. They rarely generate excitement. That lack of flash causes people to underestimate their value.

In cheer terms, this is overlooking the base because the flyer is in the air. The routine only works because the base is steady.

Bonds are not meant to impress. They are meant to support.

How Bonds Work

Bonds are loans.

When you buy a bond, you are lending money to a government or company. In return, you receive regular interest payments and the promise that your original investment will be returned at a specific time, called maturity.

That structure is predictable by design.

In cheer terms, bonds are the steady base. They do not fly. They do not twist. They hold position so the routine stays controlled.

Understanding this role makes their purpose clear. Bonds exist to reduce chaos, not to chase excitement.

Why Predictability Matters

Predictability provides confidence.

When part of your portfolio behaves in a known way, emotional pressure decreases. You are less likely to panic during market swings because not everything is moving at once.

In cheer terms, this is knowing the timing will hold even if something feels off. Predictability allows recovery.

Interest Rate Risk and Credit Risk

Bonds come with two primary risks.

Interest rate risk affects bond prices when interest rates change. When rates rise, existing bonds become less attractive. When rates fall, existing bonds become more valuable.

Credit risk reflects the borrower's ability to repay. Governments and strong companies typically carry lower credit risk. Weaker borrowers offer higher interest but increase the chance of default.

In cheer terms, this is weight and trust. Heavier stunts require more strength. Trust matters. You do not attempt difficulty beyond your preparation.

Not all bonds carry the same level of risk. Knowing the difference prevents surprises.

Why Higher Yield Usually Means Higher Risk

Higher interest payments can look attractive.

They often come with additional risk. That risk may show up during stress, not during calm periods.

In cheer terms, this is adding difficulty without improving fundamentals. It looks fine until pressure hits.

Understanding risk helps bonds play their intended role.

When Bonds Make Sense

Bonds are most valuable when stability matters.

They can reduce volatility, provide income, and act as a counterbalance to stocks. They often play a larger role as goals get closer or when income matters more than growth.

In cheer terms, this is choosing clean execution over pushing difficulty when consistency is the priority.

Timing determines fit.

Bonds are not about maximizing returns. They are about managing risk so progress stays intact.

Why Bonds Feel More Important Later

As timelines shorten, recovery time decreases.

Early in a career, volatility may be tolerable. Later, stability becomes more important. Bonds help smooth outcomes when there is less time to recover from mistakes.

In cheer terms, this is veteran leadership. Longevity matters more than flash.

Stability in a Diversified Portfolio

Diversification is about balance.

Stocks provide growth. Bonds provide stability. Cash provides flexibility. Each plays a role.

In cheer terms, this is role clarity. Every position matters. A routine fails if everyone tries to do the same thing.

Balance keeps momentum steady even when conditions change.

When one part struggles, another supports. That is the point.

Why Balanced Portfolios Feel Dull but Work

Balanced portfolios often feel boring.

Some parts lag. Others lead. Nothing feels dramatic. That boredom is often a sign the system is working.

In cheer terms, clean routines rarely feel chaotic. They feel controlled.

Stability allows discipline to stay intact.

Avoiding the "All or Nothing" Trap

Many people swing between extremes.

All stocks when markets feel good. All cash when markets feel scary. That behavior increases stress and damages results.

In cheer terms, this is changing the routine every time something feels uncomfortable. Confidence disappears.

Bonds reduce the need for extreme reactions.

Coach's Perspective

A coach would emphasize control.

Stay balanced.

Protect the routine.

Know your role.

Consistency wins.

No coach builds a routine with only difficulty. Control is what allows difficulty to work.

Bonds are about control, not excitement.

Game Situations and Decision Points

Markets feel volatile. Do you seek balance or chase returns?

You need income soon. Do you adjust or ignore timing?

Your portfolio feels dull. Do you understand why that might be a good thing?

Balance is intentional.

Common Athlete Mistakes and Financial Parallels

Athletes overvalue difficulty.

Financially, that leads to instability.

Athletes ignore balance.

Financially, that leads to stress.

Athletes misunderstand roles.

Financially, that leads to poor allocation.

Awareness corrects all three.

Why Bonds Support Discipline

Bonds help investors stay disciplined.

They reduce emotional swings. They provide predictability. They make it easier to hold growth assets during downturns.

In cheer terms, this is having a reliable base. Confidence increases when support is solid.

Discipline becomes sustainable when the routine feels controlled.

Winning the Long Game

Bonds help keep routines clean and portfolios steady.

They do not make headlines. They do not feel exciting. They quietly do their job.

That job matters.

Long-term success comes from staying upright, not from chasing difficulty at the wrong time.

Athlete Takeaways

- Bonds are loans that provide stability and structure.
- Interest rate and credit risk matter.
- Bonds make sense when stability is a priority.
- Balance reduces volatility and emotional pressure.
- Clean routines depend on control.

Chapter 13: Funds, ETFs, and Team-Based Investing

Cheer is never a solo sport.

Even when one athlete is in the air, the entire routine depends on the team. Bases, spotters, timing, and trust all work together. No one succeeds alone, and no single role carries the entire routine.

Funds and ETFs work the same way.

Instead of relying on one company, one stock, or one idea, team-based investing spreads responsibility across many parts working together. This approach reduces pressure, increases consistency, and protects against individual mistakes.

Why Solo Investing Feels Appealing but Fails Often

Many investors are drawn to picking individual winners.

They want control. They want credit. They want the excitement of being right.

In cheer terms, this is trying to carry the routine alone. It looks impressive in theory, but it increases risk dramatically.

One missed count. One slip. One injury. Everything falls apart.

Team-based investing accepts a simple truth. You do not need to be perfect to succeed. You need structure.

Mutual Funds vs ETFs

Mutual funds and ETFs both pool money from many investors to buy a diversified set of investments.

Mutual funds typically trade once per day at a set price and may require minimum investments. ETFs trade throughout the day like stocks and often allow more flexibility and lower entry points.

In cheer terms, both are team routines. The structure is slightly different, but the goal is the same. Shared responsibility and coordinated execution.

Neither option is inherently better. What matters is understanding how each fits into your routine, your schedule, and your temperament.

The choice matters less than consistency.

Why Structure Beats Customization for Most People

Many people believe customized portfolios perform better.

In reality, complexity increases decision fatigue. More decisions create more opportunities for mistakes.

In cheer terms, overly customized routines break down under pressure. Clean routines hold.

Funds and ETFs provide built-in structure that removes the need for constant decision-making.

Index vs Active Strategies

Index strategies follow a market or benchmark. They do not try to outsmart the system. They aim to capture broad market performance with minimal intervention.

Active strategies try to outperform through selection, timing, and judgment. They require more decisions and introduce more uncertainty.

Neither approach is automatically right or wrong.

In cheer terms, indexing is a clean, consistent routine. Active strategies add difficulty. Both can work, but higher difficulty increases the chance of mistakes.

Consistency often beats complexity.

Why Difficulty Increases Risk Even With Skill

Even skilled athletes miss under pressure.

Even skilled managers underperform over time.

In cheer terms, higher difficulty increases scoring potential, but it also increases fall risk. Only some teams should pursue it, and only when fundamentals are rock solid.

Indexing works because it removes ego from the equation.

Fees and Expense Ratios

Fees quietly affect outcomes.

Expense ratios are the cost of running a fund. They may look small, but over time they compound against you, reducing returns year after year.

In cheer terms, fees are like sloppy transitions. You may not notice them in the moment, but they drain momentum over time.

High fees require higher performance just to break even. Low fees preserve progress automatically.

Cost control is one of the few factors investors can control.

Why Small Costs Matter Over Long Periods

Many people ignore small percentages.

Over decades, those small percentages can mean the difference between financial flexibility and financial stress.

In cheer terms, repeated small deductions add up. Clean execution compounds.

Lower costs do not guarantee success, but higher costs guarantee a harder path.

Diversification Without Complexity

Diversification reduces risk by spreading exposure.

Funds and ETFs allow diversification across companies, industries, and regions without managing dozens of individual investments.

In cheer terms, this is trusting the system instead of trying to do everything yourself. You do not need to spot, tumble, stunt, and call counts all at once.

Simple systems are easier to maintain, especially when life gets busy.

Why Diversification Feels Boring but Works

Diversification rarely feels exciting.

Some holdings will always lag. Others will lead. That imbalance is intentional.

In cheer terms, some roles get more attention than others. All are necessary.

Diversification shows its value during stress, not during calm.

Avoiding Concentration Risk

Concentration feels confident.

Putting money into a few ideas feels decisive. It also increases vulnerability.

In cheer terms, stacking the entire routine on one athlete invites disaster.

Team-based investing accepts that no one knows the future. Spreading responsibility reduces the cost of being wrong.

Staying Disciplined With Team-Based Strategies

The hardest part of team-based investing is trust.

Trusting the system. Trusting the process. Trusting that you do not need to intervene constantly.

In cheer terms, this is trusting choreography under pressure. You stay on counts even when instincts urge you to adjust.

Discipline allows compounding to work quietly.

Coach's Perspective

A coach would reinforce teamwork.

Trust the team.

Know your role.

Avoid unnecessary flash.

Clean execution wins.

Championship routines are rarely about heroics. They are about coordination.

Team-based investing rewards discipline, patience, and humility.

Game Situations and Decision Points

You want simplicity. Do you choose structure or chase complexity?

You see performance differences. Do you understand the role of fees or chase short-term results?

You feel pressure to pick winners. Do you rely on the team or try to carry the routine alone?

The system matters more than any single decision.

Common Athlete Mistakes and Financial Parallels

Athletes try to do too much.

Financially, that leads to overtrading.

Athletes ignore fundamentals.

Financially, that leads to higher costs.

Athletes underestimate teamwork.

Financially, that leads to concentration risk.

Awareness corrects all three.

Why Team-Based Investing Builds Confidence

Team-based investing reduces pressure.

You are no longer responsible for being right every time. You are responsible for staying disciplined.

In cheer terms, shared responsibility builds confidence. You perform better knowing the team supports you.

Confidence grows when outcomes feel manageable.

Winning the Long Game

Team-based investing builds resilience.

Funds and ETFs keep routines stable, diversified, and repeatable. They allow progress to compound without requiring constant intervention.

Long-term success rarely comes from brilliance. It comes from staying consistent when others panic or overreact.

Athlete Takeaways

- Funds and ETFs spread responsibility across many investments.
- Mutual funds and ETFs differ in structure, not purpose.
- Index and active strategies serve different roles.
- Fees quietly affect long-term results.
- Diversification reduces risk without adding complexity.
- Team execution beats solo heroics.

Chapter 14: Real Estate and Alternative Paths

Not every athlete follows the same path.

In cheer, routines are built around different strengths. Some athletes specialize in stunting. Others in tumbling. Others in timing, transitions, and execution. The routine works because paths vary, not because everyone does the same thing.

Financial paths work the same way.

Real estate and alternative investments offer options beyond traditional stocks and bonds. They can play a role, but only when they fit your timing, risk tolerance, and long-term goals. These paths are tools, not trophies.

Why Real Estate and Alternatives Get Overhyped

Real estate and alternatives are often marketed as shortcuts.

Passive income. Tangible assets. Diversification. Independence.

Those benefits can be real, but the risks are often minimized or ignored. What looks stable from the outside may require significant time, capital, and emotional bandwidth.

In cheer terms, this is seeing a routine hit once on social media without seeing the injuries, missed reps, and adjustments behind it.

Context matters.

Renting vs Owning

Owning a home is often framed as a milestone. Renting is sometimes viewed as a failure.

That framing is wrong.

Renting provides flexibility. Owning provides stability and responsibility. Neither option defines success.

In cheer terms, this is role selection. You do not force an athlete into a position that does not fit their readiness or strengths. A flyer is not a base just because someone else is doing it.

Renting allows mobility, lower upfront commitment, and fewer maintenance responsibilities. Owning adds predictability, potential long-term equity, and greater responsibility.

The right choice depends on timing, location, income stability, and lifestyle goals.

Housing decisions should support your routine, not pressure it.

Why Timing Matters More Than Labels

Many people rush into ownership because they feel behind.

That pressure leads to stretched finances, reduced flexibility, and stress when life changes.

In cheer terms, this is forcing a skill before fundamentals are clean. It may work briefly, but risk increases.

Timing beats labels every time.

REITs and Indirect Ownership

Real Estate Investment Trusts allow investors to participate in real estate without owning property directly.

They provide exposure to income-producing real estate while avoiding day-to-day management, maintenance, and tenant issues. REITs can offer diversification and income within a portfolio structure.

In cheer terms, REITs are supporting roles. You contribute to the routine and benefit from the outcome without carrying the full physical load.

This indirect approach allows participation without over-commitment. It reduces complexity while still providing exposure.

REITs are not risk-free, but they often fit more easily into a diversified plan than direct ownership.

Why Ownership Is Not the Only Way to Participate

Many people believe the only "real" way to invest in real estate is to own property.

That belief ignores alternatives that may better fit their routine.

In cheer terms, not everyone needs to stunt to contribute. Supporting roles matter.

Indirect ownership can provide balance without overwhelming responsibility.

Alternatives Like Commodities and Private Investments

Alternatives include commodities, private equity, private credit, and other non-traditional investments.

These assets can add diversification, but they often come with higher risk, less transparency, limited liquidity, and complex structures.

In cheer terms, this is adding difficulty. It can work, but only when fundamentals are solid and safety is prioritized.

Alternatives are rarely appropriate as a starting point. They are enhancements, not foundations.

Before adding alternatives, core systems should already be working. Cash flow should be stable. Emergency funds should exist. Long-term goals should be clear.

Alternatives should complement, not replace, core strategies.

Why Complexity Increases Risk

Complex investments feel sophisticated.

They also reduce flexibility.

In cheer terms, this is adding layers to a routine until execution suffers. Complexity magnifies mistakes.

Simple strategies executed consistently often outperform complex ones managed emotionally.

Liquidity and Risk Considerations

Liquidity is how easily you can access money.

Real estate and many alternatives are less liquid. Selling takes time. Accessing cash may not be possible when you need it most.

That lack of flexibility increases risk if life changes unexpectedly.

In cheer terms, this is being locked into a routine. If something changes mid-season, adjustments are harder.

Liquidity matters more than returns when timing is off.

Understanding liquidity helps prevent being trapped in good investments at the wrong time.

Why Athletes Often Underestimate Liquidity Risk

Athletes are trained to commit fully.

That mindset can make illiquidity feel manageable. But financial commitments do not respond to effort the way training does.

In cheer terms, effort cannot fix structural limitations.

Liquidity provides margin. Margin provides options.

Evaluating Fit Before Adding New Paths

Before pursuing real estate or alternatives, ask fundamental questions.

Does this fit your current role and capacity?

Is the timing right?

Can you manage the responsibility emotionally and financially?

Are your core systems already stable?

In cheer terms, this is checking readiness before adding difficulty.

Not every opportunity is meant for you right now.

Coach's Perspective

A coach would slow the conversation.

Does this fit your role?

Is the timing right?

Can you manage the responsibility?

Are the basics solid?

Not every path is right for every athlete.

Discipline includes knowing when to say no.

Game Situations and Decision Points

You feel pressure to buy. Do you evaluate timing or react emotionally?

An opportunity appears. Do you assess liquidity or focus on returns?

You want diversification. Do you understand the risks or follow the crowd?

Intentional choices prevent regret.

Common Athlete Mistakes and Financial Parallels

Athletes chase roles that do not fit.

Financially, that leads to stress.

Athletes add difficulty too soon.

Financially, that leads to excessive risk.

Athletes ignore timing.
Financially, that leads to illiquidity.
Awareness corrects all three.

Winning the Long Game

Real estate and alternatives can add value when used intentionally.

When they fit your routine, they support growth and diversification. When they do not, they create imbalance and pressure.

Long-term success is not about doing everything. It is about doing what fits.

Athlete Takeaways

- Not every financial path fits every athlete.
- Renting and owning serve different purposes.
- REITs offer indirect real estate exposure with less complexity.
- Alternatives increase risk and reduce liquidity.
- Timing and fit matter more than labels.
- Choose paths that support your routine, not pressure it.

Part IV: Adjustments, Trust, and Execution

G*reat teams adjust without losing confidence.*

No routine is perfect every time.

Even the best teams make adjustments. Timing shifts. Roles change. Life intervenes. What separates strong teams from struggling ones is not the absence of mistakes. It is the ability to adjust without panic or loss of confidence.

Money works the same way.

Your financial plan is not static. Income changes. Goals evolve. Markets move. Family responsibilities grow. The ability to adjust while staying disciplined is what keeps momentum intact.

This part of the book focuses on execution under real-world conditions.

How to make changes without overreacting.

How to trust the plan while updating it.

How to stay composed when things do not go exactly as expected.

In cheer, adjustments happen quietly. They are intentional. They protect the routine without drawing attention. Financial adjustments should work the same way.

The goal is not constant change.

The goal is confident execution, steady discipline, and smart adjustments that keep everything moving forward.

Chapter 15: Asset Allocation and Balance in the Routine

Every strong cheer routine depends on balance.

If too much weight shifts in one direction, stability disappears. Even talented athletes struggle when roles are misaligned or timing is off. Balance keeps the routine controlled, confident, and repeatable.

Asset allocation plays the same role in your financial life.

It is how you divide money among different types of investments to manage risk, growth, and stability. It is not about picking winners. It is about building a routine that holds under pressure.

Why Asset Allocation Matters More Than Selection

Many people believe investment success comes from choosing the right stock or the right moment.

In reality, asset allocation explains the majority of long-term outcomes. How your money is divided matters far more than which specific investments you choose.

In cheer terms, this is choreography versus individual skills. A routine fails not because one athlete lacks talent, but because roles are unbalanced.

Allocation sets the foundation. Everything else builds on it.

Stocks, Bonds, and Cash Balance

Each component has a role.

Stocks are for growth. They bring power, momentum, and long-term potential. They also introduce volatility. Big swings are part of the job.

Bonds are for stability. They reduce volatility, smooth movement, and provide balance when conditions change.

Cash is for flexibility. It allows quick adjustments, covers short-term needs, and provides psychological stability during uncertainty.

In cheer terms, stocks are difficulty, bonds are control, and cash is spacing. A routine fails if everything leans too heavily in one direction.

A portfolio overloaded with stocks may feel exciting but becomes unstable under pressure. Too much cash feels safe but limits progress. Balance depends on how these pieces work together.

Why Overloading One Area Creates Stress

People often chase growth.

They push too much money into stocks because they want faster results. That decision increases volatility and emotional pressure. When markets dip, fear increases and discipline breaks down.

In cheer terms, this is adding difficulty before fundamentals are solid. The routine looks impressive until it does not.

Balance reduces stress, which improves decision-making.

Domestic vs International Exposure

Markets exist beyond one country.

Domestic investments tie you to familiar systems, companies, and regulations. International investments add diversification by spreading exposure across different economies, currencies, and growth cycles.

In cheer terms, this is competition experience. Teams that only perform in one environment struggle when conditions change. Exposure builds adaptability.

Geographic diversification reduces reliance on any single outcome. It does not guarantee success, but it increases resilience.

Why Familiarity Feels Safer Than It Is

People often over-invest in what feels familiar.

They recognize company names. They trust local markets. Comfort replaces strategy.

In cheer terms, this is staying in one gym and assuming competition will feel the same everywhere.

True balance includes unfamiliar elements that protect against blind spots.

Diversification Principles

Diversification means spreading risk.

It does not eliminate risk. It manages it. When one area struggles, another may stabilize the routine.

In cheer terms, diversification is role balance. You do not stack all responsibility on one athlete. You distribute it across the team so the routine holds even if one element wobbles.

Diversification works best when it is simple and consistent. Overcomplicating strategies increases confusion and emotional decision-making.

Simple diversification done consistently beats complex strategies done inconsistently.

Why Diversification Requires Patience

Diversification rarely feels exciting.

Some investments will lag at any given time. That is the point. When everything performs the same, risk concentrates.

In cheer terms, this is supporting sections that are not in the spotlight. Their role becomes obvious only when something goes wrong.

Diversification shows its value during stress, not during calm.

Career-Stage Allocation

Asset allocation changes over time.

Early stages often allow more growth-focused allocation because time absorbs volatility. You have more seasons ahead to recover from mistakes and benefit from compounding.

Later stages shift toward stability and income as goals get closer. Preservation matters more than acceleration.

In cheer terms, this is progression. Beginners focus on clean basics. Advanced athletes add difficulty when ready. Veterans protect longevity and consistency.

Your allocation should match where you are, not where someone else is.

Why Comparing Allocations Is Dangerous

People often copy others.

They hear what friends are doing. They see headlines. They follow trends without context.

In cheer terms, this is copying another team's routine without understanding their strengths or experience level.

Allocation must reflect your timeline, goals, and tolerance for pressure.

Adjusting Allocation Without Panic

Asset allocation is not static.

It evolves as life changes. Income shifts. Family responsibilities grow. Goals come closer.

Adjustments should be intentional, not emotional.

In cheer terms, this is refining choreography after evaluating film. You do not scrap the routine mid-performance. You correct deliberately.

Planned adjustments preserve confidence.

Coach's Perspective

A coach would focus on fundamentals.

Know your role.

Stay balanced.

Do not overload one side.

Adjust as you progress.

Asset allocation is about discipline, not prediction.

You do not need to know the future. You need a structure that holds in any environment.

Game Situations and Decision Points

Markets move. Do you rebalance or react emotionally?

Your life changes. Do you adjust allocation intentionally?

You compare yourself to others. Do you stay in your routine?

Balance requires confidence and self-awareness.

Common Athlete Mistakes and Financial Parallels

Athletes chase difficulty too early.

Financially, that leads to volatility.

Athletes ignore balance.

Financially, that leads to stress.

Athletes copy others.

Financially, that leads to misalignment.

Awareness corrects all three.

Why Balance Creates Freedom

Balanced routines feel controlled.

Athletes perform with confidence because the structure supports them. The same is true financially. Balanced portfolios reduce emotional swings and increase consistency.

Confidence grows when outcomes feel manageable.

Winning the Long Game

Asset allocation keeps the routine steady.

It protects against extremes. It allows growth without panic. It makes adjustments easier because the foundation is sound.

When balance is intentional, progress becomes sustainable instead of stressful.

Athlete Takeaways

- Stocks, bonds, and cash each serve a role.
- Balance matters more than chasing growth.
- Geographic diversification adds resilience.
- Diversification manages risk, not returns.
- Allocation should match your career stage.
- Balance keeps the routine clean and controlled.

Chapter 16: Buying, Holding, and Trusting the Plan

Once a routine is built, the hardest part begins.

Not learning the skills.

Not memorizing the counts.

The hardest part is trusting the routine when pressure hits.

When the crowd is loud.

When something feels off.

When instinct tells you to rush, adjust, or change something mid-performance.

Investing works the same way.

Buying and holding are simple in theory and difficult in practice. Discipline, not knowledge, determines success.

Why Execution Matters More Than Intelligence

Most people do not fail at investing because they lack intelligence.

They fail because execution breaks down under pressure.

They know they should stay consistent. They know markets move. They know long-term plans work. But when emotions spike, logic fades.

In cheer terms, this is knowing the routine perfectly but letting nerves disrupt timing when it matters most.

Execution is where results are decided.

Opening and Funding Accounts

Opening investment accounts is a mechanical step.

It can be done quickly. It can be done online. It feels productive.

Funding those accounts consistently is where progress actually happens.

In cheer terms, opening an account is joining the team. Funding it is showing up to practice. Nothing improves without reps.

Accounts that are opened but never funded do nothing. Accounts that are funded sporadically struggle to gain momentum.

Consistency creates rhythm. Rhythm creates progress.

Why Consistency Beats Timing

Many people wait for the perfect moment to invest.

They want the right market conditions. The right news. The right signal.

That moment rarely arrives.

In cheer terms, this is waiting for perfect conditions before practicing. Improvement never happens that way.

Regular contributions remove timing pressure. You are no longer guessing. You are executing.

Market Orders vs Limit Orders

Market orders execute immediately at the current price. Limit orders execute only if a specific price is reached.

Both have legitimate uses.

In cheer terms, this is choosing tempo. Sometimes you move immediately because timing matters more than precision. Sometimes you wait for the right moment to hit a transition cleanly.

The mistake is overthinking.

Order types are tools, not strategies. They support execution. They do not replace a plan.

Hesitation costs more than imperfect execution.

Why Overthinking Creates Inaction

Many people freeze because they want to avoid mistakes.

They delay. They wait. They analyze. Meanwhile, nothing happens.

In cheer terms, this is standing still between counts. Timing breaks down.

Progress requires motion, not perfection.

Buy-and-Hold Discipline

Buy-and-hold is not passive.

It is disciplined.

It means committing to a long-term plan and resisting the urge to react to short-term noise. Markets move. Emotions fluctuate. Discipline keeps you steady.

In cheer terms, this is staying on counts even when something feels slightly off. You trust the routine you trained for.

Buy-and-hold works because time does the work.

Why Buy-and-Hold Feels Uncomfortable

Buy-and-hold feels uncomfortable because it removes control in the short term.

You cannot fix every movement. You cannot adjust every fluctuation. You must trust the structure.

In cheer terms, this is trusting muscle memory instead of thinking through every motion mid-routine.

Discomfort does not mean something is wrong. It often means the plan is working.

Avoiding Emotional Decisions

Emotions are the biggest threat to execution.

Fear during downturns.

Excitement during rallies.

Comparison when others talk about wins.

These emotions pull people off their plan long before logic has a chance to intervene.

In cheer terms, this is reacting to crowd noise instead of music cues.

Emotional decisions break routines and portfolios.

Why Emotion Feels So Convincing

Emotions feel urgent.

They demand action now. They create stories. They justify deviation.

In cheer terms, this is adrenaline convincing you to rush a count.

Pausing is a skill.

The ability to do nothing is often the most valuable investing skill.

Trusting the Plan When It Feels Wrong

Every long-term plan will feel wrong at some point.

Markets will drop. Headlines will sound alarming. Others will claim better results.

This is not a flaw in the plan. It is part of the process.

In cheer terms, this is the moment when fatigue sets in and execution must carry you through.

Trust is built before pressure arrives.

Coach's Perspective

A coach would reinforce trust.

Stick to the plan.

Do not panic.

Execute what you trained.

Finish strong.

Confidence does not come from improvising. It comes from preparation.

Game Situations and Decision Points

Markets drop. Do you hold or sell?

Markets rise. Do you chase or stay disciplined?

You feel unsure. Do you trust the plan or abandon it?

These decisions feel small in the moment. They define outcomes over time.

Execution defines results.

Common Athlete Mistakes and Financial Parallels

Athletes second-guess routines.

Financially, that leads to poor timing.

Athletes overreact to mistakes.

Financially, that leads to emotional trades.

Athletes lose trust under pressure.

Financially, that leads to inconsistency.

Discipline corrects all three.

Why Stillness Is a Skill

Doing nothing feels irresponsible.

But often, doing nothing is the correct action.

In cheer terms, holding a position requires strength and control. Movement is not always progress.

In investing, stillness allows compounding to work.

Winning the Long Game

Buying and holding require discipline, not brilliance.

They reward patience, consistency, and trust. When execution stays clean under pressure, compounding does the heavy lifting.

The difference between long-term success and short-term stress is rarely intelligence. It is behavior.

Strong routines finish clean because athletes trust what they trained.

Strong portfolios grow because investors trust what they built.

Athlete Takeaways

- Consistent funding matters more than perfect timing.
- Opening accounts is easy. Funding them builds momentum.
- Order types are tools, not strategies.
- Buy-and-hold rewards patience.
- Emotions disrupt execution.
- Trust the plan and stay on counts.

Chapter 17: Rebalancing and Mid-Season Adjustments

No cheer season runs exactly as planned.

Athletes get stronger. Roles change. Injuries happen. Timing improves in some areas and slips in others. Strong teams do not panic when adjustments are needed. They review, correct, and move forward without losing confidence.

Rebalancing works the same way in investing.

It is not about fixing mistakes. It is about maintaining balance as conditions change. Rebalancing protects your original game plan while allowing growth to continue.

Why Rebalancing Feels Uncomfortable

Rebalancing often feels counterintuitive.

It asks you to trim what is doing well and add to what is not. Emotionally, this feels wrong. Psychologically, people want to chase what is winning and abandon what is lagging.

In cheer terms, this is letting one section rush because it feels strong while ignoring another that needs support. The routine becomes unbalanced even though effort remains high.

Discipline means doing what works, not what feels good.

How Often to Review Investments

Constant checking creates anxiety.

Markets move daily. Headlines amplify every swing. Checking too often invites emotion into decisions. On the other hand, rarely checking allows drift to accumulate unnoticed.

The goal is periodic review.

In cheer terms, this is film review. You do not watch film after every count. You review consistently enough to identify patterns and correct issues before they become problems.

For most people, reviewing investments once or twice a year is enough. More frequent reviews are only helpful when life circumstances change.

Consistency beats obsession.

Why Too Much Monitoring Hurts Performance

Excessive monitoring increases emotional reactions.

Small fluctuations feel bigger. Confidence wavers. Decision-making becomes reactive instead of intentional.

In cheer terms, this is watching the routine too closely mid-performance. Overthinking disrupts flow.

Rebalancing works best when it is planned, not triggered by fear or excitement.

Rebalancing Strategies

Rebalancing means adjusting your portfolio back to its intended mix.

Over time, different investments grow at different rates. Some outpace expectations. Others lag temporarily. Rebalancing restores balance by trimming what has grown too large and reinforcing what has fallen behind.

In cheer terms, this is correcting timing. You slow down what is rushing and support what is falling behind.

This process enforces discipline automatically. It removes emotion from the decision. You are not guessing. You are executing a plan.

Why Rebalancing Protects You From Yourself

Left alone, portfolios drift toward risk.

The best performers grow larger. Risk increases quietly. Then volatility feels worse because exposure is higher than intended.

In cheer terms, this is pushing difficulty without adjusting technique. Eventually the risk catches up.

Rebalancing resets risk before it becomes a problem.

Life Changes and Portfolio Updates

Markets are not the only reason to adjust.

Life changes require updates too.

New jobs. Income changes. Family responsibilities. Health considerations. Time horizon shifts. These all affect your financial routine.

In cheer terms, this is updating choreography when the team changes. You do not force old roles to fit new realities.

Ignoring life changes creates misalignment. Plans should evolve as life evolves.

Why Athletes Often Resist Updating Plans

Athletes are trained to push through.

That mindset can create resistance to adjustment. Some people stick to outdated plans because change feels like failure.

In cheer terms, this is keeping a routine that no longer fits the team. Effort stays high, but performance suffers.

Updating a plan is not quitting. It is adapting.

Avoiding Over-Adjustment

Too much adjustment can be as harmful as none.

Constant tinkering introduces instability. It increases stress and reduces confidence. Small changes compound into confusion.

In cheer terms, this is changing choreography too often. Athletes lose rhythm. Execution suffers.

Adjust intentionally, not emotionally.

A plan that is changed too often becomes a guess, not a strategy.

Why Simplicity Supports Discipline

Simple plans are easier to maintain.

Complex strategies invite second-guessing. Simplicity reduces decision fatigue and increases consistency.

In cheer terms, clean routines outperform flashy ones under pressure.

Rebalancing works best when the process is clear and repeatable.

Coach's Perspective

A coach would guide calmly.

Review.

Adjust when needed.

Do not overcorrect.

Trust the process.

Mid-season discipline wins championships.

The goal is not perfection. The goal is consistency.

Game Situations and Decision Points

Markets move. Do you rebalance or react emotionally?

Life changes. Do you update the plan or ignore it?

You feel uncertain. Do you simplify or complicate?

Adjustment requires clarity, not urgency.

Common Athlete Mistakes and Financial Parallels

Athletes overcorrect mistakes.

Financially, that leads to instability.

Athletes avoid review.

Financially, that leads to drift.

Athletes panic mid-season.

Financially, that leads to poor timing.

Awareness corrects all three.

Why Rebalancing Builds Confidence

Rebalancing creates control.

You are no longer reacting to markets or guessing outcomes. You are executing a process.

In cheer terms, this is trusting your counts even when the crowd is loud.

Confidence comes from preparation.

A disciplined process reduces anxiety.

Winning the Long Game

Rebalancing keeps routines clean and portfolios aligned.

It protects progress while allowing growth. Smart adjustments preserve confidence and momentum without sacrificing discipline.

Strong teams do not fear adjustments. They respect them.

Athlete Takeaways

- Review investments periodically, not constantly.
- Rebalancing restores balance and manages risk.
- Life changes require plan updates.

- Over-adjustment creates instability.
- Clean corrections keep the routine strong.

Chapter 18: The Mental Side of Money

The hardest part of cheer is not physical.

It is mental.

Pressure. Expectations. Comparison. Crowd noise. One mistake can shake confidence if you let it. The athletes who perform best are not the ones who never feel pressure. They are the ones who know how to manage it.

Money brings the same mental challenges.

Most financial mistakes are not caused by lack of knowledge. They are caused by emotion. Fear, overconfidence, comparison, and pressure quietly influence decisions long before logic gets involved.

Understanding the mental side of money is not optional. It is foundational.

Why Mental Discipline Matters More Than Technical Knowledge

Many people assume financial success comes from knowing the right answers.

In reality, most people already know the basics. Spend less than you earn. Save consistently. Avoid high-interest debt. Stay patient.

The challenge is execution under pressure.

In cheer terms, this is knowing the routine but struggling to hit it when the lights come on. Knowledge exists. Composure wavers.

Mental discipline is what allows good habits to show up consistently.

Pressure, Confidence, and Comparison

Pressure shows up in different forms.

Pressure to keep up.

Pressure to make the right move.

Pressure to prove you are doing well.

Comparison magnifies pressure. Seeing others talk about wins, income, or lifestyle can make you question your own progress.

In cheer terms, this is watching another team hit a routine before you go on. If you let it get in your head, timing slips and confidence fades.

Comparison rarely provides useful information. It only introduces doubt.

Confidence does not come from outperforming others. It comes from preparation and repetition. Financial confidence is built by knowing your plan and trusting your reps, even when others appear to be ahead.

Why Comparison Is Especially Dangerous With Money

Money comparisons are incomplete.

You see outcomes, not tradeoffs. You see highlights, not stress. You see results, not risk.

In cheer terms, this is judging a routine without seeing practice. It looks effortless, but you do not see the hours behind it.

Comparing incomplete information leads to misaligned decisions.

Crowd Noise and Expectations

The crowd is loud in cheer.

Judges. Teammates. Coaches. Spectators. Noise is constant. Athletes are trained to block it out and focus on counts and cues.

Money has its own crowd noise.

News headlines. Social media. Friends. Family. Opinions everywhere. Predictions, warnings, hype, fear. Most of it is not relevant to your situation.

In cheer terms, reacting to noise instead of music leads to missed counts.

Financially, reacting to noise leads to poor decisions.

The louder the noise, the more important the plan becomes.

Why Emotional Reactions Are Costly

Emotional decisions feel urgent.

They demand action now. They bypass reflection. They often feel justified in the moment and regrettable later.

In cheer terms, this is forcing a skill mid-routine because the crowd reacts. The risk increases immediately.

Pausing is a skill.

Building Systems for Discipline

Discipline fades when it relies on willpower.

Willpower fluctuates. Emotions change. Motivation rises and falls. Systems protect discipline when motivation drops.

Automation. Rules. Check-ins. Boundaries. These systems remove emotion from decisions.

In cheer terms, this is choreography. You do not decide what to do mid-routine. You execute what was planned.

Systems turn good intentions into repeatable behavior.

Why Systems Beat Motivation Every Time

Motivation feels powerful but unstable.

Systems feel boring but reliable.

In cheer terms, clean reps beat hype. Fundamentals outperform intensity over time.

Financial systems create consistency when emotions would otherwise interfere.

Staying Composed After Mistakes

Mistakes will happen.

An overspend. A missed savings goal. A poor decision. What matters is the response.

Overreacting compounds damage. Ignoring mistakes allows patterns to form.

In cheer terms, one missed count does not end a routine unless you panic. Panic creates additional errors. Composure allows recovery.

Financial composure follows the same rule. Correct, learn, and move forward.

Why Shame Makes Things Worse

Many people respond to financial mistakes with shame.

Shame leads to avoidance. Avoidance leads to repetition.

In cheer terms, this is refusing to review film after a mistake. The error remains uncorrected.

Mistakes are feedback, not verdicts.

Coach's Perspective

A coach would ground you.

Control what you can control.

Block out the noise.

Trust your preparation.

Next count.

Mental discipline separates strong performers from inconsistent ones.

No routine is perfect. Composure keeps it intact.

Game Situations and Decision Points

You see others doing better. Do you compare or stay focused on your plan?

You make a mistake. Do you spiral or reset?

You feel pressure to act. Do you pause or rush?

These moments are not dramatic. They are decisive.

Mental choices shape outcomes long before results appear.

Common Athlete Mistakes and Financial Parallels

Athletes compare instead of focusing.

Financially, that leads to misaligned decisions.

Athletes react emotionally.

Financially, that leads to poor timing.

Athletes lose composure after mistakes.

Financially, that leads to compounding errors.

Awareness corrects all three.

Why Calm Is a Competitive Advantage

Calm allows clarity.

Clarity allows consistency.

Consistency builds progress.

In cheer terms, calm performers hit routines others miss. In finances, calm decision-makers outperform reactive ones over time.

You do not need to feel confident. You need to act consistently.

Winning the Long Game

Mental discipline protects consistency.

When you control emotion, build systems, and stay composed, progress continues even through setbacks. Confidence grows from execution, not perfection.

The goal is not to eliminate emotion.
The goal is to prevent emotion from driving decisions.

Athlete Takeaways

- Pressure and comparison distort decisions.
- Crowd noise is constant. Focus on your counts.
- Systems protect discipline when motivation fades.
- Mistakes require correction, not panic.
- Composure keeps the routine intact.

Part V: Life Beyond the Mat

Cheer does not last forever.

The mat clears. The season ends. The uniform gets put away. What remains are the habits, mindset, and discipline you built along the way.

Life beyond the mat brings new responsibilities. Careers. Families. Financial decisions that stretch across decades, not just seasons. The structure changes, but the need for discipline does not.

This part of the book focuses on applying what you have learned to real life.

Taxes. Careers. Housing. Family dynamics. Long-term planning. These chapters address decisions that shape stability well beyond athletics. There are no judges and no music cues here. Accountability becomes internal.

Just like cheer, success after the mat depends on preparation, communication, and trust in your process. The routines are different, but the principles are the same.

Life beyond the mat is where consistency matters most.

Chapter 19: Taxes and Where You Place Your Energy

In cheer, energy matters.

Where you place it determines how the routine feels. Waste energy early and you struggle later. Use it intentionally and the routine finishes strong, controlled, and confident.

Taxes work the same way.

You cannot avoid them entirely, but you can decide where to place your energy and attention. Understanding how taxes interact with your money allows more of your effort to actually count instead of leaking away quietly.

Taxes are not just a once-a-year event. They touch every paycheck, every investment decision, and every long-term plan.

Why Taxes Feel Overwhelming to Many Athletes

For many athletes, taxes feel intimidating.

They show up with unfamiliar language, deadlines, and rules that seem designed to confuse. That discomfort leads to avoidance. Avoidance leads to missed opportunities and unnecessary stress.

In cheer terms, this is ignoring technique because it feels technical. You can still perform for a while, but inefficiencies add up.

Taxes are not about being perfect. They are about being intentional.

Taxable vs Tax-Advantaged Accounts

Taxable accounts are flexible.

You can access money at any time. There are no penalties for withdrawals. That flexibility comes with a cost. Taxes apply as you earn income, receive interest, or realize investment gains.

Tax-advantaged accounts offer benefits such as deferring or eliminating taxes, often in exchange for restrictions around access or timing.

In cheer terms, taxable accounts are open practice. Tax-advantaged accounts are structured training. Both matter, but they serve different roles.

Flexibility without structure wastes energy. Structure without flexibility creates rigidity. Balance creates efficiency.

Using the right account for the right purpose increases the effectiveness of every dollar you earn.

Why Account Choice Matters More Than Most People Realize

Many people focus on what they invest in.

Far fewer focus on where those investments live.

Two people can earn the same return and end up with very different results based solely on taxes. That difference compounds over time.

In cheer terms, this is two teams with the same skills but different execution. The outcome depends on efficiency.

Tax-Deferred vs Tax-Free Growth

Tax-deferred growth postpones taxes until later. You receive benefits now, but taxes are paid when money is withdrawn.

Tax-free growth avoids taxes entirely if rules are followed. You pay taxes upfront, then future growth belongs to you.

Neither option is automatically better.

In cheer terms, this is pacing. Sometimes you conserve energy early so you can finish strong later. Sometimes you invest energy early to reduce strain at the end.

The right choice depends on income, life stage, and future expectations. Understanding the difference allows you to place energy where it works hardest.

Why Timing Matters More Than Prediction

Many people try to predict future tax rates.

That approach creates paralysis.

Instead of predicting perfectly, focus on diversification across tax treatments. Having a mix of taxable, tax-deferred, and tax-free assets provides flexibility regardless of what changes.

In cheer terms, this is building a routine that adapts under pressure.

Asset Location Basics

Asset location is about where investments are held, not what investments you own.

Some assets generate more taxable income. Others grow quietly. Placing them in appropriate accounts reduces unnecessary tax drag.

In cheer terms, this is positioning. You place athletes where they perform best. You do not randomly assign roles.

Small adjustments here can make a significant difference over time without changing your investment strategy.

Efficiency compounds just like growth.

Why Small Tax Drags Matter

Tax drag often feels invisible.

It does not show up as a single bill. It shows up as slower progress.

Over years and decades, that drag can cost more than poor investment selection.

In cheer terms, this is sloppy transitions. Nothing looks broken, but the routine loses sharpness.

Common Tax Mistakes

A few mistakes show up repeatedly.

Ignoring taxes until filing time.

Using the wrong accounts for long-term goals.

Overlooking the impact of small, ongoing tax drags.

Avoiding planning because taxes feel complicated.

These mistakes are not about intelligence. They are about avoidance.

Most people do not fail at taxes. They disengage from them.

Awareness reduces frustration and restores control.

Why Avoidance Is the Most Expensive Strategy

Avoidance feels easier in the moment.

But it creates surprises later. Higher bills. Missed opportunities. Regret over decisions that could have been adjusted earlier.

In cheer terms, this is skipping review because practice feels long. The mistakes show up at competition.

Coach's Perspective

A coach would remind you.

Be intentional.

Do not waste energy.

Plan ahead.

Finish strong.

No coach ignores where energy is spent. Taxes are simply another place where efficiency matters.

Preparation reduces stress.

Game Situations and Decision Points

You earn more. Do you adjust your tax strategy or ignore the change?

You invest. Do you consider account placement or default to convenience?

You feel overwhelmed. Do you seek clarity or avoid the topic entirely?

Where you place energy determines outcomes.

Common Athlete Mistakes and Financial Parallels

Athletes waste energy early.

Financially, that leads to higher taxes.

Athletes ignore positioning.

Financially, that leads to inefficiency.

Athletes avoid uncomfortable topics.

Financially, that leads to surprises.

Awareness corrects all three.

Why Tax Planning Is Ongoing, Not Annual

Taxes are not a once-a-year event.

They are part of daily decisions. Saving. Investing. Career changes. Big purchases. Planning early allows adjustments before consequences lock in.

In cheer terms, this is monitoring energy throughout the routine, not just at the end.

Winning the Long Game

Tax awareness allows your effort to go further.

When you understand where to place your energy, progress compounds instead of leaking away. You keep more of what you earn. Stress decreases. Confidence increases.

Taxes will always exist. Waste does not have to.

Athlete Takeaways

- Taxes affect every financial decision.
- Tax-advantaged accounts increase efficiency.
- Tax-deferred and tax-free growth serve different roles.
- Asset location reduces unnecessary drag.
- Planning beats avoidance.
- Intentional energy finishes strong.

Chapter 20: Retirement Accounts and Financial Independence

In cheer, routines are built with the ending in mind.

You do not pour everything into the opening counts and hope you have something left. You pace yourself. You manage energy. You plan transitions so the routine finishes strong, not sloppy.

Retirement planning works the same way.

Financial independence is not about one big moment or one perfect decision. It is about building systems over time that allow you choices later. Retirement accounts provide the structure that makes that possible.

Why Retirement Feels Abstract to Many Athletes

For many athletes, retirement feels distant.

The word itself sounds like stopping, slowing down, or becoming irrelevant. That framing makes it easy to ignore, especially early in a career when income feels uncertain and life feels busy.

In cheer terms, this is ignoring the dismount because competition feels far away. The routine looks fine early, but the finish determines the final impression.

Retirement planning is not about age.

It is about options.

The earlier structure is built, the more flexible life becomes later.

Employer Plans and Pensions

Employer-sponsored plans are often the foundation of retirement planning.

401(k)s and similar plans allow you to save automatically through your paycheck. This removes decision-making and builds consistency. Some employers offer matching contributions, which is essentially free support added to your routine.

Pensions are less common today, but when available, they provide guaranteed income later in life. That reliability reduces pressure on other savings.

In cheer terms, this is team support. When the program provides structure, using it strengthens the routine. Ignoring it means leaving support unused.

Automatic saving works because it turns discipline into a system. You do not have to feel motivated. You just show up.

Why Athletes Often Delay Participation

Many former athletes delay participating in employer plans.

They plan to start later. They feel income is too tight. They underestimate how quickly time passes.

In cheer terms, this is skipping early conditioning because competition feels far away. That decision always shows up later.

Participation matters more than perfection. Starting small beats waiting for ideal conditions.

Traditional and Roth IRAs

IRAs give you additional control beyond employer plans.

Traditional IRAs generally offer tax benefits upfront. Roth IRAs offer tax benefits later. The difference is about when taxes are paid, not whether they exist.

In cheer terms, this is energy management. Sometimes you conserve energy early. Sometimes you push earlier so the finish is cleaner.

The right choice depends on income, tax expectations, and long-term goals. There is no universally correct option. There is only what fits your situation.

What matters most is consistency. Accounts work when they are used repeatedly over time.

Contribution and Withdrawal Rules

Retirement accounts come with rules.

Contribution limits exist. Withdrawal timing matters. Penalties apply if rules are ignored. These rules are not meant to punish. They are designed to encourage long-term behavior.

In cheer terms, this is routine structure. Counts exist for a reason. Ignoring them creates mistakes that affect the entire performance.

Understanding the rules prevents frustration and costly errors. Most mistakes happen not because people are reckless, but because they are uninformed or rushed.

Structure protects discipline.

Why Rules Actually Create Freedom

Rules often feel restrictive.

But in reality, they create freedom by removing ambiguity. When you know the boundaries, decisions become easier.

In cheer terms, structure allows creativity within the routine. Without counts, nothing flows.

Retirement account rules exist to keep you focused on the long game.

Retirement Income Basics

Retirement is not about stopping.

It is about shifting.

Income may come from multiple sources. Employer plans. Personal savings. Investment accounts. Possibly pensions or other benefits. The goal is reliability and flexibility, not inactivity.

In cheer terms, this is the dismount. You want control, balance, and confidence. You do not want panic at the end of the routine.

Planning early allows income streams to work together instead of compete. It reduces reliance on any single source.

Why Athletes Often Underestimate the Finish

Athletes are trained to focus on the present rep.

That focus can make it difficult to think decades ahead. But retirement planning rewards those who respect the finish.

In cheer terms, this is treating the final counts as an afterthought. The routine may be strong, but the ending determines the outcome.

The finish deserves as much attention as the opening.

Coach's Perspective

A coach would think long-term.

Plan the whole routine.

Use available support.

Follow the structure.

Finish strong.

No coach builds a routine without considering the ending.

Retirement planning rewards patience and consistency, not intensity.

Game Situations and Decision Points

You have access to a plan. Do you participate or delay?

You earn more. Do you increase contributions or increase spending?

You want flexibility later. Do you build structure now?

Early decisions compound quietly.

Common Athlete Mistakes and Financial Parallels

Athletes burn energy too early.

Financially, that leads to under-saving.

Athletes ignore structure.

Financially, that leads to penalties.

Athletes underestimate the finish.

Financially, that leads to stress later.

Awareness corrects all three.

Why Consistency Beats Big Moves

Many people think retirement requires big contributions or perfect timing.

In reality, consistency matters more than intensity. Small, steady contributions over time outperform sporadic large efforts.

In cheer terms, clean reps beat occasional full-out performances.

Systems beat motivation.

Winning the Long Game

Retirement accounts turn discipline into independence.

They allow today's effort to support tomorrow's freedom. They convert consistency into options. When used intentionally, they make financial independence achievable instead of abstract.

The goal is not to retire early or stop working.

The goal is to control choices.

Athlete Takeaways

- Employer plans provide built-in structure and support.
- Traditional and Roth IRAs manage taxes at different times.
- Rules exist to protect long-term goals.
- Retirement income is about reliability, not stopping.

- Plan the finish from the beginning.

Chapter 21: Housing and Major Financial Decisions

Big decisions change the feel of the entire routine.

In cheer, adding a new stunt, transition, or sequence affects timing, spacing, and trust across the team. Even when the skill looks exciting, it changes how everyone moves. Major financial decisions work the same way.

Housing, vehicles, and large purchases influence cash flow, flexibility, stress levels, and long-term stability. They do not exist in isolation. They touch everything else in your financial routine.

These choices deserve intention, not pressure.

Why Big Purchases Feel So Heavy

Major purchases feel different because they last.

Unlike everyday spending, housing and vehicles follow you for years. They create fixed obligations that must be met regardless of income changes, life transitions, or unexpected events.

In cheer terms, this is committing to a routine you must perform every time you take the mat. Once it is set, it cannot be ignored.

Pressure often comes from outside sources. Friends buying homes. Social media showing upgrades. Family expectations. Lenders approving you for more than you planned.

Approval does not equal readiness.

Renting vs Buying

Renting and buying are tools, not trophies.

Renting offers flexibility, lower responsibility, and fewer long-term commitments. Buying offers stability, potential equity, and a sense of permanence. Neither option defines success.

In cheer terms, this is choosing the right role. You do not force a position that does not fit your readiness, timing, or life stage. You choose what allows the routine to work cleanly.

Timing matters more than labels.

Buying too early can create stress. Renting too long without purpose can stall progress. The right decision depends on stability, goals, and personal readiness, not comparison.

Why Athletes Often Feel Pressure to Buy

Former athletes are used to progression.

Move up levels. Increase difficulty. Advance roles. That mindset can translate into feeling behind if life does not follow a clear upward path.

Buying a home can feel like a visible marker of adulthood or success.

In cheer terms, this is equating difficulty with progress. But clean execution matters more than forcing a skill before you are ready.

Housing should support your routine, not dominate it.

Mortgages and Down Payments

A mortgage is a long-term commitment.

It affects monthly cash flow, risk exposure, and flexibility. The size of the down payment plays a major role in how much pressure that commitment creates.

Larger down payments reduce monthly strain and risk. Smaller down payments increase leverage and vulnerability.

In cheer terms, this is load management. Too much weight without enough support increases injury risk. Balance protects the routine.

Understanding loan terms, interest rates, and affordability matters more than chasing the biggest purchase you qualify for.

Qualification is not a recommendation. It is a maximum.

Why Affordability Is About More Than the Payment

Many people focus only on the monthly payment.

That is incomplete.

Housing includes taxes, insurance, maintenance, utilities, and unexpected repairs. Ignoring those factors creates false confidence.

In cheer terms, this is judging a stunt by how it looks once, not how it feels over an entire routine.

Affordability is about sustainability, not approval.

Cars, Leases, and Financing Traps

Vehicles are necessary for many people.

They provide access to work, family, and opportunity. But they are also one of the most common sources of financial strain.

Financing and leasing create convenience, but they also introduce risk. Long terms, high interest rates, and frequent upgrades quietly drain cash flow.

In cheer terms, this is overusing equipment. Just because something is available does not mean it fits your routine.

Transportation should support your life, not strain it.

Reliable transportation that fits your budget is success. Flashy upgrades that limit flexibility are not.

Why Vehicles Become Silent Budget Killers

Cars depreciate.

They lose value while payments remain fixed. When terms are extended and upgrades are frequent, cash flow becomes locked into something that provides no long-term return.

In cheer terms, this is investing energy into a move that does not score higher but costs more effort.

Awareness prevents regret.

Planning Major Purchases

Large purchases should be planned, not rushed.

Impulse decisions often feel justified in the moment. Pressure. Excitement. Fear of missing out. Those emotions fade quickly. The commitment does not.

Planning allows you to assess timing, impact, and tradeoffs.

In cheer terms, this is walk-through before full-out. You review counts, spacing, and transitions before committing to maximum effort.

Preparation prevents mistakes that are expensive to undo.

Why Slowing Down Is a Strength

Many former athletes struggle with slowing down.

They associate urgency with performance. But adult financial decisions reward patience more than speed.

In cheer terms, this is learning when to control tempo instead of pushing intensity.

Pausing does not mean you are behind. It means you are intentional.

Coach's Perspective

A coach would slow you down.

Check readiness.

Understand the commitment.

Do not rush under pressure.

Protect long-term stability.

Big decisions affect everything else in the routine.

No coach adds difficulty without confirming the team is ready.

Game Situations and Decision Points

You feel pressure to buy. Do you pause or rush?

You qualify for financing. Do you assess affordability or trust approval?

You want something now. Do you plan or react emotionally?

These moments define whether decisions support momentum or create drag.

Common Athlete Mistakes and Financial Parallels

Athletes rush difficulty.

Financially, that leads to overcommitment.

Athletes ignore timing.

Financially, that leads to stress.

Athletes chase appearances.

Financially, that leads to regret.

Progress feels good. Stability lasts longer.

Winning the Long Game

Housing and major purchases shape your financial routine.

They influence stress, flexibility, and opportunity for years. When decisions are intentional, stability follows. When they are rushed, pressure builds and options shrink.

Just like cheer, clean execution beats forced difficulty.

The goal is not to impress.

The goal is to sustain.

Athlete Takeaways

- Renting and buying serve different purposes.
- Mortgages are long-term commitments.
- Down payments affect risk and flexibility.
- Vehicles should support, not strain, cash flow.
- Planning reduces regret.
- Big decisions deserve patience.

Chapter 22: Your Career Is a Team Effort

No cheer routine succeeds on individual effort alone.

Even the most talented athlete depends on timing, support, trust, and coordination from others. One person may carry a stunt, but the routine only works when everyone understands their role and executes together.

Careers work the same way.

Success is rarely about one job, one paycheck, or one decision. It is about how all the pieces work together over time. Salary, benefits, growth opportunities, flexibility, and sustainability all matter.

Your career is your primary engine for financial stability. Treating it intentionally matters.

Salary vs Total Compensation

Salary is only part of the picture.

Total compensation includes bonuses, retirement contributions, health insurance, disability coverage, paid time off, flexibility, career development, and long-term growth opportunities. Focusing only on salary can lead to decisions that look good upfront but fall short over time.

In cheer terms, salary is one stunt. Total compensation is the entire routine. You do not judge a performance based on one moment. You evaluate timing, execution, safety, and flow.

A higher salary with weak benefits may reduce stability. A slightly lower salary with strong benefits may create more long-term value. Understanding total compensation allows you to compare opportunities accurately instead of emotionally.

Many former athletes struggle here because they were trained to focus on the most visible metric. In careers, the most visible number is rarely the most important one.

Job Changes and Benefits

Changing jobs can be a powerful move.

It can increase income, flexibility, or satisfaction. It can also reset benefits, disrupt stability, and introduce risk if not planned carefully.

Health insurance matters. Retirement plans matter. Matching contributions matter. Vesting schedules matter. Paid time off matters. Losing or gaining benefits changes the entire routine.

In cheer terms, this is changing teams mid-season. It can work, but it requires adjustment. New systems. New expectations. New timing.

Intentional transitions protect momentum. Reactive transitions often create setbacks.

Before making a move, ask what you gain and what you lose. Careers are not just ladders. They are ecosystems.

Why Athletes Often Underestimate Benefits

Athletes are trained to push through discomfort.

That mindset can cause people to overlook benefits because they feel secondary to performance or income. Over time, ignoring benefits increases stress, risk, and burnout.

In cheer terms, this is ignoring safety protocols because the routine feels clean. Everything works until it does not.

Benefits protect consistency. Consistency supports long-term success.

Negotiation Basics

Negotiation is uncomfortable for many people.

That discomfort leads to avoidance, and avoidance costs money over time. Negotiation does not require confrontation. It requires preparation, clarity, and confidence.

In cheer terms, this is advocating for the routine. You speak up to protect timing, safety, and execution. You are not being difficult. You are being responsible.

Negotiation can involve salary, responsibilities, flexibility, benefits, growth paths, or timing. Asking questions is not demanding. It is due diligence.

Understanding your value and communicating it clearly creates better outcomes. Silence rarely benefits you.

Why Athletes Avoid Negotiation

Many former athletes were trained to earn roles, not ask for them.

They waited for coaches to decide. That model does not translate well to careers. Waiting often results in missed opportunities.

In cheer terms, this is standing in position waiting for music that never starts.

Negotiation is not entitlement. It is communication.

Side Income and Entrepreneurship

Side income can add flexibility and opportunity.

It can also add complexity, time pressure, and risk. Not every opportunity fits your routine or your current capacity.

In cheer terms, this is adding an extra role. It can strengthen the team if it fits. It can disrupt everything if it overloads the routine.

Side income should support long-term goals, not distract from them. Ask whether the opportunity aligns with your time, energy, and priorities.

Entrepreneurship is not required for success. It is a tool, not a mandate.

Avoiding the Hustle Trap

Many athletes feel pressure to always do more.

Side projects. Extra work. Constant hustle. That pressure can lead to burnout if not aligned with purpose.

In cheer terms, this is training nonstop without recovery. Performance eventually drops.

Balance protects longevity.

Coach's Perspective

A coach would emphasize teamwork.

Know your role.

Communicate clearly.

Prepare before stepping into something new.

Protect consistency.

Careers are built through coordination, not isolation.

Strong performers understand how their role fits into the larger system.

Game Situations and Decision Points

You receive an offer. Do you evaluate total compensation or focus only on salary?

You feel underpaid. Do you prepare for negotiation or avoid it?

An opportunity appears. Do you assess fit or chase it impulsively?

Career decisions shape financial outcomes long before paychecks arrive.

Common Athlete Mistakes and Financial Parallels

Athletes focus on one moment.

Financially, that leads to narrow decisions.

Athletes avoid hard conversations.

Financially, that leads to missed opportunities.

Athletes overload the routine.

Financially, that leads to burnout.

Awareness corrects all three.

Why Coordination Matters More Than Speed

Some careers grow fast and collapse.

Others grow steadily and compound.

In cheer terms, clean execution beats rushed difficulty. Timing and coordination create stability.

When salary, benefits, growth, and balance work together, stress decreases and confidence increases. You are no longer reacting. You are building.

Winning the Long Game

Strong careers are built intentionally.

They are not about constant movement. They are about aligned movement. When compensation, benefits, communication, and purpose support each other, progress compounds over time.

Treat your career like a team effort.

You do not have to do everything yourself. You just have to coordinate well.

Athlete Takeaways

- Salary is only part of compensation.
- Benefits affect long-term stability.
- Negotiation requires preparation, not aggression.
- Side income should fit your routine.
- Careers succeed through coordination and clarity.

Chapter 23: Estate Planning Basics Everyone Needs

Estate planning is not about age or wealth.

It is about responsibility.

In cheer, safety plans exist long before anything goes wrong. Spotters know their roles. Emergency protocols are practiced. Communication is clear. No one waits for an injury to decide who does what. Preparation protects everyone involved, even if it is never needed.

Estate planning serves the same purpose in your financial life.

It is not pessimistic. It is protective. It is leadership expressed quietly, behind the scenes, so that when pressure is high, confusion is low.

Why Estate Planning Feels So Uncomfortable

Most people avoid estate planning because it forces uncomfortable thoughts.

Loss. Incapacity. Hard conversations. Uncertainty. None of these are pleasant to think about, especially when life feels busy, healthy, and normal. Avoidance feels easier than preparation.

But avoiding planning does not avoid outcomes.

It only shifts stress, confusion, and decision-making onto the people you care about most. Loved ones are left guessing what you wanted, who should decide, and how things should be handled, often while they are already overwhelmed.

In cheer terms, this is skipping safety walkthroughs because they feel awkward.

Everything might be fine. Until it is not.

Planning is not an act of fear. It is an act of care.

What Estate Planning Actually Is

Estate planning is not just about what happens after death.

It also addresses what happens if you are alive but unable to make decisions for yourself. Illness, injury, or unexpected events can remove your ability to communicate clearly long before end-of-life situations are involved.

A good estate plan answers simple but critical questions:

- Who makes decisions if you cannot?
- Who receives what, and when?
- Who is responsible for carrying out your wishes?
- How do things transfer smoothly instead of creating conflict?

Estate planning creates structure where emotion would otherwise take over.

Wills and Trusts: Structure, Not Status

A will outlines what happens to your assets and who is responsible for carrying out your wishes.

It allows you to name guardians for children, assign an executor, and clearly state how property and belongings should be handled. Without a will, state laws decide for you, regardless of whether those decisions align with your intentions.

Trusts can provide additional control, privacy, and protection depending on your situation.

They are often useful when:

- There are minor children
- There are blended families

- There are concerns about timing, responsibility, or protection of assets
- Privacy matters
- Simpler transfer is desired

Not everyone needs a complex structure.

Everyone needs clarity.

In cheer terms, this is choreography.

Without choreography, people guess. Guessing leads to missed timing, confusion, and mistakes. A routine does not need to be complicated to work. It needs to be clear.

A basic plan is better than no plan. Perfection is not required. Intention is.

Why "I'll Do It Later" Is Risky

Many people tell themselves they will handle estate planning later.

Later when they are older.

Later when they have more assets.

Later when life slows down.

The problem is that life rarely slows down on its own. And unexpected events do not wait for ideal timing.

Estate planning is not about predicting the future. It is about acknowledging that uncertainty exists and choosing not to leave others unprotected because of it.

In cheer, no team waits until competition day to assign spotters.

Preparation happens before it feels necessary.

Beneficiaries and Account Titling: Where Plans Often Break

One of the biggest misconceptions about estate planning is believing that a will controls everything.

Many assets pass outside of a will.

Retirement accounts, life insurance policies, and certain bank and investment accounts transfer based on beneficiary designations. Account titling determines ownership and control. These rules override what a will says.

That means your estate plan can look perfect on paper and still fail in practice.

In cheer terms, this is alignment.

If people are not in the right place on the mat, timing breaks down even if the routine was designed well. Everyone might think they know what should happen, but execution fails.

Keeping beneficiaries updated is one of the simplest and most important steps you can take.

Yet it is one of the most commonly overlooked.

Life changes. Relationships evolve. People pass away. Children grow up. Your documents should evolve too.

How Small Oversights Create Big Problems

Many estate issues are not caused by lack of planning.

They are caused by incomplete planning.

An ex-spouse still listed as beneficiary.

A parent named years ago who can no longer serve.

Accounts titled inconsistently across institutions.

Documents that conflict with each other.

In cheer terms, this is forgetting to update counts after changing choreography.

The routine looks familiar, so no one questions it. Then execution fails because people are following different versions of the plan.

Small details matter.

And the cost of fixing them is far lower before something happens than after.

Powers of Attorney: Protecting Decision-Making

Powers of attorney allow someone you trust to act on your behalf if you cannot.

This includes financial and legal decisions. Paying bills. Managing accounts. Signing documents. Handling obligations. Without these documents, loved ones may face delays, court involvement, and additional stress during already difficult moments.

In cheer terms, this is leadership coverage.

When a captain is unavailable, someone else steps in. Roles are clear. Authority is understood. Action is possible.

Without clarity, everything slows down.

Choosing the right person matters more than choosing the perfect document. Trust, reliability, and communication are essential. A technically correct document is useless if the wrong person is named.

Preparation reduces chaos.

Healthcare Directives: Clarity During Emotional Moments

Healthcare directives communicate your wishes for medical care.

They guide decisions when you cannot speak for yourself. They also relieve loved ones from guessing what you would want while they are under emotional strain.

In cheer terms, this is emergency planning.

You hope it is never needed. But when it is, clarity matters more than optimism. Healthcare decisions are deeply personal. Documenting them protects both your autonomy and your family.

It is not about controlling every outcome. It is about reducing uncertainty when emotions are high.

Estate Planning Is Really About People, Not Assets

Estate planning is often framed as a financial exercise.

In reality, it is relational.

It reduces conflict.

It prevents confusion.

It protects loved ones from unnecessary stress.

In cheer terms, this is protecting the team.

You plan so others do not have to scramble when pressure is high. You remove ambiguity so people can focus on supporting each other instead of arguing about what should happen.

The goal is not control.

The goal is care.

Why Avoidance Creates Conflict

When plans are unclear, people fill gaps with assumptions.

Those assumptions are influenced by grief, stress, and emotion. Disagreements arise not because people are bad, but because they are unsure. Estate disputes often damage relationships far more than finances.

Avoidance feels easier today.

It costs more tomorrow.

Coach's Perspective on Responsibility

A coach would not avoid this conversation.

Plan ahead.

Protect the team.

Remove uncertainty.

Handle responsibility.

No coach waits for injury to assign spotters. Leadership means preparing for uncomfortable scenarios so others are protected.

Estate planning is leadership.

It is taking responsibility for outcomes that affect others, even when you may not be there to manage them.

Game Situations and Decision Points

Estate planning shows up at quiet moments, not dramatic ones.

You think you have time. Do you act now or delay?

Your life changes. Do you update documents or assume they still work?

You assume someone knows your wishes. Do you confirm or hope?

Clarity prevents stress. Delay multiplies it.

Estate Planning Is Not One-and-Done

Estate planning is not a single event.

It is a process.

Marriage. Children. Divorce. Career changes. Moves. Health updates. Asset growth. Each transition is a cue to review documents.

In cheer terms, this is updating routines as skills and teams change.

You do not keep old choreography when the team evolves. Reviewing plans does not mean something is wrong. It means you are paying attention.

Regular reviews keep plans relevant and effective.

Why Early Planning Is an Advantage

Planning early does not mean expecting the worst.

It means reducing the cost of uncertainty.

When plans are in place:

- Decisions happen faster
- Stress is lower
- Conflict is reduced
- Loved ones are protected

You do not need to be wealthy. You do not need complex structures. You need clarity.

Winning the Long Game

Estate planning protects more than assets.

It protects people.

When plans are clear, loved ones can focus on healing instead of guessing. They can support each other instead of navigating confusion. They can move forward with confidence instead of conflict.

Just like cheer, preparation behind the scenes allows performance under pressure.

Athlete Takeaways

Estate planning is about responsibility, not wealth.

Discomfort is a signal to prepare, not avoid.

Wills and trusts create structure and clarity.

Beneficiaries and account titling must align.

Powers of attorney and healthcare directives protect loved ones.

Estate planning is leadership in action.

Strong teams prepare before pressure hits.

Strong financial lives do the same.

Chapter 24: Talking About Money With Family

Money conversations are rarely about money.

They are about expectations, emotions, responsibility, and trust. That is why they feel uncomfortable for so many people. Numbers are simple. Relationships are not.

In cheer, communication matters just as much as technique. You can have perfect skills, but if communication breaks down, timing suffers and mistakes multiply. A clean routine depends on clear signals, trust, and shared understanding.

Family finances work the same way.

Avoiding conversations does not prevent problems.

It delays them.

Why Money Feels Harder to Talk About at Home

Family history follows money.

Past sacrifices. Unspoken expectations. Power dynamics. Guilt. Pride. Fear. These emotions show up quietly in financial conversations, even when no one names them.

Many people avoid these conversations because they do not want conflict. Others avoid them because they fear disappointing someone. The result is the same.

Silence.

In cheer terms, this is skipping communication because the routine feels tense. Everyone hopes things work out, but no one addresses the timing issue until something breaks.

Clear communication prevents damage.

Teaching Kids About Money

Kids learn money habits long before they understand money concepts.

They watch how you spend, save, react, and plan. They notice stress. They notice avoidance. They notice priorities.

What you model matters more than what you explain.

In cheer terms, this is demonstration. You do not just tell athletes how to perform. You show them. Your habits become the lesson.

Simple lessons go a long way.

Delayed gratification.

Saving for goals.

Understanding tradeoffs.

Learning that choices have consequences.

These skills build confidence and responsibility early. They also remove fear. Money becomes something to manage, not something to avoid.

You do not need perfect answers. You need consistency.

Supporting Parents and Caregivers

As life progresses, roles often reverse.

Parents age. Needs change. Health issues arise. Caregiving becomes part of the routine. These transitions bring emotional and financial complexity that few people are prepared for.

In cheer terms, this is role adjustment.

When a teammate is injured, others step up. The routine changes. Responsibilities shift. Support requires communication and planning.

Family caregiving works the same way. Without discussion, assumptions form. Without planning, stress multiplies. Without boundaries, resentment builds.

Understanding finances early helps avoid crisis-driven decisions later.

Why Avoidance Creates More Stress Over Time

Many families avoid financial conversations until something forces them.

A medical event. A job loss. A sudden need for support. By then, emotions are high and options are limited.

In cheer terms, this is adjusting the routine during competition instead of practice. Pressure increases and mistakes become more likely.

Early conversations create flexibility. Late conversations create urgency.

Setting Boundaries and Expectations

Boundaries protect relationships.

Helping family financially without clarity often leads to resentment, confusion, or dependency. Even when intentions are good, lack of structure causes strain.

In cheer terms, boundaries are spacing. Without it, collisions happen. Everyone may be trying to help, but the routine falls apart.

Clear boundaries answer important questions.

What can I help with?

What can I not help with?

Is this temporary or ongoing?

What expectations exist on both sides?

Support should be intentional, not reactive.

Boundaries do not mean saying no to people. They mean saying yes to clarity.

Navigating Financial Conversations

Money conversations feel heavy because stakes feel personal.

People tie money to worth, effort, and sacrifice. That makes discussions emotional even when the topic is practical.

Approach these conversations with curiosity instead of judgment.

Ask questions.

Listen without interrupting.

Be clear about what you can and cannot do.

In cheer terms, this is communication under pressure. Calm voices keep routines clean. Emotional reactions create mistakes.

You do not need perfect words.

You need honesty and respect.

Why Timing Matters in Family Conversations

Timing affects outcomes.

Trying to talk about money during conflict rarely works. Waiting until there is a crisis also limits options.

In cheer terms, this is choosing the right moment to make adjustments. Mid-routine chaos is not ideal.

Choose calm moments. Plan conversations. Treat them like important practices, not emergency drills.

Coach's Perspective

A coach would stress communication.

Talk early.

Be clear.

Respect roles.

Protect relationships.

Silence creates more problems than difficult conversations.

Avoidance feels easier. Communication is more effective.

Game Situations and Decision Points

A family member asks for help. Do you pause or react emotionally?

A child has questions. Do you avoid the topic or engage?

Tension arises. Do you clarify expectations or ignore them?

Communication determines outcomes long before money does.

Common Athlete Mistakes and Financial Parallels

Athletes avoid tough conversations.

Financially, that leads to misunderstandings.

Athletes overextend themselves to help the team.

Financially, that leads to resentment.

Athletes assume everyone is aligned.

Financially, that leads to conflict.

Clear communication prevents all three.

Replacing Assumptions With Clarity

Many family conflicts are not caused by money.

They are caused by assumptions.

Assumptions about responsibility.

Assumptions about fairness.

Assumptions about intentions.

In cheer terms, this is assuming timing instead of counting. Eventually, someone is off.

Clarity replaces assumptions. Conversations create clarity.

Winning the Long Game

Healthy financial conversations strengthen relationships.

When expectations are clear and communication is respectful, money becomes a tool instead of a source of tension. Families feel safer. Decisions feel shared instead of forced.

Just like cheer, strong routines rely on trust and communication, not silence.

Athlete Takeaways

- Kids learn money habits through observation.
- Family roles change over time.
- Boundaries protect relationships.
- Honest conversations reduce stress.
- Communication keeps the routine together.

Part VI: Finishing Strong Together

Every cheer routine is remembered by the finish.

No matter how clean the opening counts were or how difficult the stunts became, the ending sets the tone. Strong teams finish with control, confidence, and unity. They stay connected through the final count.

Finishing strong financially works the same way.

Long-term success is not about one decision or one season. It is about consistency, support, and accountability over time. No one builds lasting stability alone. Coaches, teammates, mentors, and trusted professionals all play a role.

This final part of the book focuses on staying connected, seeking the right help, and protecting progress as life evolves. It emphasizes avoiding common traps, recognizing bad advice, and building habits that last beyond motivation.

Just like cheer, strong finishes come from trust, preparation, and teamwork.

You do not have to do everything yourself.

Finishing strong together means knowing when to lead, when to follow, and when to ask for support.

Chapter 25: Advisors, Scams, and Long-Term Success

No strong cheer program operates without support.

Behind every successful routine is a team of coaches, trainers, and staff whose job is to keep athletes safe, focused, and progressing. The best athletes are not the ones who try to do everything alone. They are the ones who know when to ask for help and who to trust.

Financial success works the same way.

Knowing when to seek guidance and how to avoid bad advice protects everything you have worked to build.

When to Seek Professional Help

There is no single moment that requires professional help.

Instead, it is transitions that usually trigger the need. New income. Job changes. Marriage. Buying a home. Starting a business. Receiving an inheritance. Navigating complex tax situations.

In cheer terms, this is increasing difficulty.

When routines become more complex, support increases. You do not add advanced stunts without additional spotters. You do not increase risk without preparation.

Seeking help is not a sign of weakness.

It is a sign of responsibility.

Many people wait too long because they believe they should already know what to do. That belief often leads to mistakes that could have been avoided with early guidance.

Types of Financial Advisors

Not all advisors serve the same role.

Some focus primarily on investments. Others focus on comprehensive planning. Some are sales-driven. Others are advice-driven. Some are paid through commissions. Others are paid directly by clients.

In cheer terms, this is role clarity.

You would not ask a tumbling coach to spot a stunt they are not trained for. You would not ask a choreographer to handle safety protocols outside their expertise. Each role matters, but only when used correctly.

Understanding how advisors are compensated and what services they actually provide matters. Compensation influences behavior. Clarity protects you.

The goal is not to find an advisor who promises the most. The goal is to find one who fits your needs, communicates clearly, and earns trust over time.

Recognizing Scams and Bad Advice

Scams prey on urgency and emotion.

Promises of guaranteed returns. Pressure to act quickly. Claims that opportunities are exclusive or time-sensitive. Lack of transparency. These are warning signs.

Bad advice often sounds confident but ignores your specific situation. It may be generic, overly aggressive, or disconnected from your goals.

In cheer terms, this is being rushed into throwing a skill without prep. When someone tells you there is no time to practice, review, or ask questions, risk increases.

Trust requires verification.

Slowing down, asking questions, and understanding details protects you far more than reacting quickly.

Why Athletes Are Often Targeted

Athletes are attractive targets.

They are disciplined. They trust authority. They are used to following confident leadership. Scammers know this.

Many athletes are also experiencing income changes for the first time. That combination creates vulnerability.

In cheer terms, this is being placed into a routine with unfamiliar counts. Confidence without context can lead to mistakes.

Awareness reduces risk.

Ten Common Financial Mistakes

Most financial mistakes are not caused by lack of intelligence.

They are caused by inaction, emotion, or misplaced trust.

1. Avoiding planning
2. Overspending lifestyle increases
3. Ignoring insurance and protection
4. Carrying high-interest debt
5. Chasing hype and trends
6. Emotional investing
7. Skipping retirement contributions
8. Failing to adjust plans as life changes
9. Avoiding difficult financial conversations
10. Waiting too long to start

These mistakes compound quietly. Rarely does one decision cause failure. It is repeated small choices that create stress later.

Ten Rules for Long-Term Success

Long-term success is built on fundamentals.

These rules are simple, not easy.

1. Live below your means
2. Automate good habits
3. Protect what you build
4. Stay diversified
5. Keep costs low
6. Be patient
7. Adjust intentionally
8. Ask for help when needed
9. Ignore noise
10. Stay consistent

In cheer terms, these are fundamentals. You do them every practice, not just on competition day.

Consistency makes them powerful.

Why Consistency Matters More Than Intensity

Many athletes struggle after sports because they confuse intensity with progress.

They try to fix everything at once. Overcorrect. Burn out. Quit.

In cheer terms, this is going full-out every rep instead of building consistency.

Financial success is built through steady execution, not dramatic moves. Showing up matters more than occasional bursts of effort.

Coach's Perspective

A coach would emphasize accountability.

Get the right help.

Avoid shortcuts.

Trust preparation.

Finish strong.

No championship routine is built on improvisation. Preparation creates confidence.

Long-term success is built through discipline and support, not isolation.

Game Situations and Decision Points

You feel overwhelmed. Do you ask for help or avoid the problem?

You hear about a great opportunity. Do you slow down or rush in?

You are unsure who to trust. Do you ask questions or stay silent?

These moments shape outcomes more than big decisions ever will.

Replacing Ego With Systems

Many former athletes struggle because asking for help feels uncomfortable.

They are used to being capable. Self-reliant. Tough.

But independence does not mean isolation.

In cheer terms, this is refusing a spot because you think you should be able to handle it. That mindset increases risk.

Strong systems reduce the need for heroics.

Winning the Long Game

Financial success is not about perfection.

It is about awareness, preparation, and steady execution over time. With the right team, clear rules, and discipline, progress compounds and stress fades.

Just like cheer, the goal is not to avoid mistakes entirely. It is to minimize risk, recover quickly, and stay in the routine.

Athlete Takeaways

- Seeking help is part of leadership.
- Not all advisors serve the same role.
- Scams rely on urgency and emotion.
- Most financial mistakes are preventable.
- Long-term success comes from consistency.

Chapter 26: Losing the Schedule and Rebuilding Structure

One of the hardest adjustments after cheer is not physical.

It is structural.

For years, your calendar was not optional. Practice times were set. Conditioning was scheduled. Travel was planned. Meetings, warm-ups, walk-throughs, and recovery all had a place. Someone else designed the structure and enforced it. Your responsibility was clear. Show up. Be on time. Execute.

Then it stops.

No warning. No gradual transition. One season ends, and suddenly your time belongs entirely to you. No coach. No posted schedule. No mandatory reps. No one checking attendance.

At first, that freedom feels incredible.

You can sleep in. You can skip a workout. You can move tasks to tomorrow. You can decide later. But over time, that freedom starts to feel heavy. What once felt like flexibility slowly becomes drift.

This is one of the most underappreciated challenges former cheerleaders face.

Why Life Gets Harder When No One Is Setting Your Calendar

Without a set schedule, discipline becomes optional.

There is no coach checking attendance. No teammate relying on you to be on time. No one asking why you skipped a workout, missed a meeting, or delayed a financial task. Budgeting, reviewing accounts, saving, planning ahead, all become things you can do later.

Later becomes tomorrow.

Tomorrow becomes next week.

Next week becomes never.

In cheer terms, this is open practice without counts.

Everyone moves. Everyone is busy. But timing disappears quickly. Skills stop syncing. Progress stalls. Nothing looks obviously broken at first, but the routine slowly loses cohesion.

Structure creates momentum.

Its absence creates drift.

Drift does not feel dangerous in the moment. It feels like freedom. Over time, it quietly erodes progress.

From Mandatory Workouts to Optional Discipline

In cheer, discipline is built into the system.

Miss practice and you lose reps. Skip conditioning and performance suffers immediately. Consequences are fast and visible. Feedback is constant. You know right away when something is off.

In adult life, skipping financial habits rarely creates instant consequences.

You skip reviewing your accounts. Nothing explodes.

You delay saving this month. Bills still get paid.

You ignore planning. Life keeps moving.

That delay is what makes optional discipline so dangerous.

You do not feel the impact today. You feel it months or years later, when savings are behind, stress is higher, and options are limited. By then, the gap feels overwhelming, even though it was created slowly.

Optional discipline is harder than mandatory discipline because no one is watching.

You must choose consistency without external pressure. You must show up when there is no immediate consequence for not doing so.

How Lack of Structure Quietly Breaks Financial Habits

Without structure, habits fade.

Saving becomes inconsistent.

Bills get paid late or just in time.

Planning gets postponed.

Goals lose urgency.

Nothing dramatic happens. There is no obvious failure point. Progress just slows. Stress increases. Confidence erodes.

In cheer terms, this is losing timing without falling.

The routine still runs. No one crashes. But everyone feels it. The performance feels rushed, uneven, and tense. Eventually, something breaks under pressure.

Most financial setbacks after sports are not caused by bad decisions.

They are caused by delayed decisions.

Why Athletes Underestimate Structural Loss

Athletes are trained for intensity, not autonomy.

You were trained to push hard when told to push hard. You were trained to show up when scheduled. You were trained to perform under pressure. You were rarely trained to design your own systems.

After cheer, many former athletes assume discipline will carry over automatically.

But discipline without structure is fragile.

In cheer terms, this is assuming performance will stay sharp without practice plans, counts, or repetition. Skill fades without intentional maintenance. Timing disappears without routine.

Structure was doing more work for you than you realized.

Replacing Practice Schedules With Personal Systems

Structure does not disappear forever.

It must be rebuilt intentionally.

Not through motivation.

Not through willpower.

Through systems.

Systems do the work when motivation fades.

Examples of financial systems include:

- Automatic transfers that save before spending
- Scheduled financial check-ins on your calendar
- Reminders that remove reliance on memory
- Rules that eliminate daily decision-making

In cheer terms, this is self-coached training.

You design the routine. You set the counts. You decide what matters. You hold yourself accountable without external enforcement.

Systems replace motivation.

Motivation fades.

Systems hold.

The goal is not to feel disciplined.

The goal is to make discipline unavoidable.

Why Freedom Without Structure Is Risky

Freedom feels like progress.

You can do anything. You can decide later. You can change plans anytime. But freedom without structure creates indecision. Indecision leads to avoidance. Avoidance leads to drift.

In cheer terms, this is unlimited floor time with no routine planned.

Everyone is moving. No one is progressing. Energy is spent without direction. Effort does not translate into improvement.

Structure does not limit freedom.

It protects it.

When systems handle the basics, your energy is freed for growth instead of cleanup. You stop reacting and start executing.

The Hidden Cost of Drift

Drift is expensive.

Not immediately. Quietly.

Missed compounding.

Delayed saving.

Higher stress.

Fewer options.

Drift does not announce itself. It accumulates. By the time it is obvious, rebuilding feels overwhelming.

Former athletes often blame themselves when this happens.

They think they lost discipline. They think something is wrong with them. In reality, they lost structure.

Discipline was never the problem.

Coach's Perspective on Life After Structure

A coach would be blunt.

No one is coming to fix this for you.

Discipline is your responsibility now.

Build structure or drift.

This is not punishment.

It is adulthood.

Coaches do not provide structure to control athletes. They provide it to produce results. Once external structure disappears, internal systems must replace it.

Game Situations and Decision Points

This transition shows up in quiet moments.

You have flexibility. Do you use it intentionally or let it dissolve?

You skip a habit. Do you reset or quit entirely?

No one is watching. Do you show up anyway?

These moments feel small.

They are not.

Structure determines outcomes long before results appear.

Common Athlete Mistakes and Financial Parallels

Athletes rely on external accountability.

Financially, that leads to inconsistency.

Athletes underestimate drift.

Financially, that leads to lost progress.

Athletes avoid systems because they feel boring.

Financially, that leads to chaos.

Discipline without systems eventually breaks.

Rebuilding Structure Without Overcorrecting

Some former athletes respond by overcorrecting.

They create extreme routines.

Overly rigid schedules.

Burnout-level systems that collapse under real life.

This is understandable. Athletes are used to intensity.

But structure should support life, not dominate it.

In cheer terms, this is over-choreographing a routine until it loses flow. Precision matters, but flexibility matters too.

Effective systems are:

- Simple

- Repeatable
- Forgiving

Miss a rep. Reset.

Miss a week. Restart.

Miss a month. Rebuild.

Progress resumes through consistency, not perfection.

Designing a Post-Cheer Structure That Works

The most effective personal systems share common traits.

They are scheduled, not optional.

They are automated where possible.

They reduce daily decisions.

They are reviewed, not ignored.

Examples:

- A monthly money check-in on your calendar
- Automatic savings that happen without thought
- A weekly reset time to review priorities
- Clear rules that prevent impulse decisions

This is not about being strict.

It is about being intentional.

Why Structure Restores Confidence

When structure returns, confidence follows.

Progress becomes predictable.

Stress decreases.

Momentum builds.

You stop wondering if you are falling behind because you can see your system working. Just like in cheer, confidence comes from preparation, not hope.

Winning the Long Game

Rebuilding structure is essential after sports.

When systems replace schedules, discipline returns. Financial stability becomes sustainable instead of reactive. Confidence grows because progress becomes predictable.

This is where former athletes regain control.

Not through intensity.

Through design.

Athlete Takeaways

Structure disappears after cheer.

Optional discipline is harder than mandatory discipline.

Lack of structure erodes habits quietly.

Systems replace motivation.

Simple systems beat extreme routines.

Build structure or drift.

You were never weak.

You were trained inside a system.

Build a new one, and discipline comes back.

Chapter 27: From Teammates to Coworkers

The transition from cheer to the workplace can feel disorienting.

In cheer, roles are clear. Coaches give direction. Expectations are known. Feedback is immediate. Film shows exactly what went right or wrong. Accountability is built into the environment from the moment you walk into the gym.

You know where to stand. You know what you are responsible for. You know when you missed a count and when you nailed it.

Most workplaces do not function that way.

Why the Workplace Feels Foreign After Sports

Athletes are trained in structure.

Your schedule was not optional. Practices had start times. Conditioning was mandatory. Performance standards were visible and enforced. When something went wrong, it was addressed quickly.

When that structure disappears, frustration builds.

In the workplace, expectations are often implied instead of stated. Performance is evaluated inconsistently. Feedback may arrive months later, or not at all. Success is not always clearly defined, and effort does not always translate directly into recognition.

In cheer terms, this is performing without counts or music. You are moving, but you are not sure whether your timing is right. You are working hard, but you do not know if you are executing what actually matters.

That uncertainty affects confidence. It creates hesitation. It can slowly erode motivation, especially for people who are used to clear standards and immediate correction.

Many former athletes are not struggling because they lack discipline. They are struggling because the system changed and no one explained the new rules.

Authority Without Coaches

In sports, authority is visible.

Coaches lead. Captains reinforce expectations. Leadership is defined. Direction is clear, even when it is tough.

In the workplace, authority can be far less obvious.

Titles do not always reflect influence. The person who makes decisions is not always the person with the highest rank. Advancement may depend on relationships, timing, or perception, not just performance.

In cheer terms, this is having no clear captain. Direction exists, but it is not consistently communicated. You are expected to read the room, interpret cues, and adjust without being told.

This can feel uncomfortable for athletes who are used to direct leadership. It can also feel unfair. But understanding this shift is critical.

Workplace authority is often informal. Learning where decisions are actually made helps reduce frustration and confusion. It also allows you to focus effort where it matters most.

Feedback Without Film

Athletes rely on film because it removes emotion.

Film shows reality. It does not argue. It does not sugarcoat. It simply shows what happened.

In many workplaces, feedback is subjective, delayed, or absent. Silence is often mistaken for approval. Praise may be vague. Criticism may arrive unexpectedly and without context.

In cheer terms, this is practicing without review. You assume things are fine until something breaks or a mistake suddenly matters more than you expected.

Former athletes often wait for feedback because that is how sports worked. In adult life, waiting can stall growth.

Seeking feedback proactively replaces missing film. Asking questions, checking alignment, and requesting clarity restores control. It turns ambiguity into information.

Feedback does not always come to you anymore. Sometimes you have to go get it.

Politics, Ambiguity, and Unclear Expectations

Workplaces include dynamics athletes are rarely trained for.

Politics. Unspoken rules. Conflicting priorities. Shifting standards. These factors influence advancement just as much as effort and skill.

In cheer terms, this is competing without knowing the judging criteria. Execution matters, but interpretation varies. Two routines can look similar and receive very different outcomes.

Many former athletes reject workplace politics because it feels dishonest or distracting. But avoiding these dynamics entirely does not make them disappear. It just removes you from the conversation.

Learning how to navigate ambiguity is not selling out. It is a career skill.

Understanding how decisions are made, what leaders value, and how priorities shift allows you to position yourself intentionally instead of reactively.

How This Impacts Income Growth and Career Stability

Uncertainty slows income growth.

Missed feedback delays improvement. Misunderstood expectations stall advancement. Avoiding workplace dynamics entirely can limit opportunity, even when performance is strong.

In cheer terms, this is staying on the mat but never increasing difficulty. You are performing, but not progressing.

Many former athletes work hard for years without seeing financial movement because they assume effort alone will be recognized. In adult careers, visibility, communication, and alignment matter just as much as output.

Career awareness directly supports financial stability. When you understand how growth actually happens, income becomes more predictable and intentional.

Coach's Perspective

A coach would reframe the challenge.

Learn the system.

Ask for clarity.

Seek feedback.

Adapt without losing discipline.

The game changed.

The work ethic did not.

Your discipline still matters. Your preparation still matters. But they must be applied differently now.

Game Situations and Decision Points

You receive little feedback. Do you assume or ask?

You feel overlooked. Do you disengage or clarify expectations?

The rules feel unclear. Do you learn them or ignore them?

These moments seem small, but they shape long-term outcomes. Adaptation determines growth.

Common Athlete Mistakes and Financial Parallels

Athletes expect structure to appear.

Financially, that leads to stalled income.

Athletes avoid workplace politics entirely.

Financially, that limits opportunity.

Athletes wait to be coached.

Financially, that slows progress.

These are not character flaws. They are transition gaps.

Winning the Long Game

Success after sports requires adjustment.

When you replace coaches with self-advocacy and teammates with collaboration, career stability improves and income growth follows. Discipline still matters, but it must be self-directed and strategically applied.

The workplace is not worse than sports. It is just different.

Those who learn the new rules early gain an advantage that compounds over time.

Athlete Takeaways

- Workplaces lack the structure athletes expect.
- Authority and feedback look different after sports.
- Ambiguity affects advancement.
- Proactive communication replaces missing film.
- Adaptation supports long-term career success.

Chapter 28: When No One Is Watching Anymore

In cheer, someone is always watching.

Coaches track effort. Teammates notice missed reps. Judges evaluate execution. The crowd reacts instantly. Accountability is constant and visible. You know when you are on. You know when you are off. That environment shapes behavior in powerful ways because effort is never private.

Then one day, it disappears.

No one is tracking your effort.

No one is checking your habits.

No one is reviewing film on your financial decisions.

There is no whistle when you skip a rep. No correction when timing slips. No immediate feedback when you delay something important. That sudden absence creates a discipline gap many former athletes do not expect and are not prepared for.

This chapter is about understanding that gap and learning how to close it.

The Discipline Gap After Accountability Disappears

External accountability drives consistency.

Schedules. Expectations. Consequences. These forces made discipline automatic. You did not have to negotiate with yourself every day. You followed the structure that already existed. When accountability is removed, habits weaken unless internal systems replace it.

Discipline that once came from outside pressure becomes optional.

In cheer terms, this is practicing alone without mirrors, music, or spotters. You can still train, but every rep requires more intention. There is no built-in correction. You must notice mistakes yourself. You must choose to care even when no one else sees the effort.

Without structure, discipline does not collapse overnight.

It fades quietly.

That quiet fade is what catches former athletes off guard. Nothing dramatic happens. Life continues. Bills get paid. Work gets done. But the edge dulls. Small habits loosen. Focus softens. Over time, that erosion becomes visible in outcomes.

Why Former Athletes Self-Sabotage Without Pressure

Pressure sharpens focus.

Competition deadlines. Practice times. Performance expectations. These conditions force clarity. Decisions get made quickly. Effort is channeled toward specific outcomes.

Without pressure, comfort creeps in.

Short-term decisions feel harmless. Skipped habits seem insignificant. Delaying something important feels reasonable because nothing bad happens immediately. That is the danger.

In cheer terms, this is lowering intensity because no one is watching.

The routine does not fall apart right away. It just loses sharpness. Timing drifts. Motions soften. Energy drops. If no one intervenes, the routine eventually becomes unrecognizable.

Self-sabotage is rarely intentional.

Former athletes are not choosing to fail. They are responding to an environment with no feedback loop. Habits go unmonitored. Decisions go unchecked. Comfort fills the space where accountability used to live.

Comfort vs Growth Decisions

Growth is uncomfortable.

It requires effort without immediate reward. It requires doing things that do not feel urgent. It requires saying no when no one would notice if you said yes.

Comfort feels safe.

Without external pressure, comfort usually wins. That choice shows up financially in predictable ways.

Overspending because it feels good now.

Under-saving because it does not feel urgent.

Delayed planning because it feels overwhelming.

Avoidance because nothing is forcing action.

In cheer terms, this is choosing easy counts instead of progressing difficulty.

The routine stays clean. Nothing crashes. But it stops improving. Over time, other teams pass you. Not because they are more talented, but because they kept progressing when you stayed comfortable.

Growth requires choosing discomfort even when no one forces you to.

That is the shift former athletes must learn to make.

Translating Grind Culture Into Adult Life

Athletes know how to grind.

Long practices. Early mornings. Physical fatigue. Mental focus. You were trained to push through discomfort and keep going. That skill does not disappear after cheer.

The problem is direction.

Grind without structure leads to burnout. Adult life does not reward constant intensity. It rewards consistent, purposeful effort applied to the right things.

In cheer terms, this is training smart instead of training nonstop.

Quality reps matter more than endless reps. Rest matters. Recovery matters. Intentional practice beats mindless effort.

Financial discipline works the same way.

Constant stress is not the goal. Constant vigilance is not sustainable. The goal is systems that quietly produce results without requiring daily heroics.

Discipline must become intentional, not reactive.

Why Money Mistakes Show Up Years Later

Financial mistakes are delayed.

Skipping saving today feels harmless. Avoiding planning feels fine. Overspending once or twice does not cause collapse. The impact shows up years later when options are limited, stress is higher, and recovery feels harder.

In cheer terms, this is poor fundamentals appearing at competition.

The mistake did not happen that day. It happened weeks earlier in practice. It happened when counts were rushed. When reps were skipped. When corrections were ignored.

Time reveals habits.

Money is unforgiving in this way. It does not punish immediately. It records patterns and reveals them later. By the time the result is visible, the cause is often forgotten.

Accountability Did Not Disappear. It Changed.

This is a critical reframing.

Accountability did not vanish after cheer. It shifted from external to internal. The scoreboard is no longer public. The feedback loop is slower. But accountability still exists.

It just shows up as outcomes instead of corrections.

Stress instead of whistles.

Limited options instead of missed reps.

Regret instead of immediate feedback.

Internal accountability requires a different skill set.

You must notice patterns early.

You must correct without being told.

You must care before consequences arrive.

This is harder than external accountability, but it is also more powerful.

Coach's Perspective on Life Without Observers

A coach would be honest.

No one is watching now.

That is the test.

Discipline is internal.

Choose growth anyway.

Coaches know that the best athletes are not the ones who perform only when observed. They are the ones who train correctly when no one is watching.

That is where championships are built.

Adult life works the same way.

Building Internal Accountability Systems

Internal accountability does not come from motivation.

Motivation fades. Willpower fluctuates. Emotion is unreliable. Systems create consistency when feelings do not cooperate.

Effective internal accountability systems include:

Scheduled reviews that happen whether you feel like it or not.

Automation that removes daily decisions.

Clear rules that reduce negotiation with yourself.

Visible tracking that replaces external observation.

In cheer terms, this is using mirrors, counts, and video when practicing alone.

You create feedback where none naturally exists.

The goal is not to feel watched. The goal is to make behavior visible to yourself.

The Role of Identity in Discipline

Former athletes often struggle because their identity was tied to external validation.

Performance was praised. Effort was noticed. Progress was acknowledged. When that disappears, effort can feel pointless.

This is where identity must evolve.

Discipline becomes about who you are, not who is watching.

You show up because that is what you do.

You save because that is how you operate.

You plan because that is part of your standard.

Identity-based discipline is quieter, but it is stronger.

Game Situations and Decision Points

The real test shows up in small moments.

You have flexibility. Do you build structure or let it dissolve?

You feel comfortable. Do you push or settle?

You skip a habit. Do you reset or ignore it?

You notice drift. Do you correct or rationalize it?

These moments do not feel dramatic.

They are not.

But they define outcomes over time.

Common Athlete Mistakes and Financial Parallels

Athletes rely on pressure to perform.

Financially, that leads to inconsistency once pressure is gone.

Athletes confuse comfort with success.

Financially, that leads to stagnation.

Athletes grind without direction.

Financially, that leads to burnout instead of progress.

The solution is not more effort.

It is better structure.

Why Direction Matters More Than Intensity

Intensity feels productive.

Sweating feels like work. Stress feels like effort. Busyness feels like progress. But without direction, intensity produces motion, not results.

In cheer, intensity without timing creates chaos.

In life, intensity without structure creates burnout.

Direction focuses effort. Systems sustain it.

Replacing External Pressure With Personal Standards

The most successful former athletes develop personal standards.

Not goals. Standards.

Standards answer the question, what do I do even when no one is watching?

I review my finances monthly.

I save consistently.

I plan ahead instead of reacting.

I correct drift early.

Standards remove debate.

They turn discipline into default behavior instead of a daily decision.

The Quiet Power of Boring Consistency

Consistency is boring.

It does not feel heroic. It does not get applause. It does not create dramatic stories. But it works.

In cheer, the best teams are built in boring practices.

In life, the best financial outcomes are built in boring habits.

Boring is not weak.

Boring is reliable.

Winning the Long Game

When no one is watching, habits matter most.

Replacing external pressure with internal systems allows discipline to continue and progress to compound. Structure becomes self-built instead of enforced. Accountability becomes internal instead of imposed.

This is where real growth begins.

Not when effort is observed.

When effort is chosen.

Athlete Takeaways

Accountability changes after sports.

Discipline must become internal.

Comfort slows growth.

Direction matters more than grind.

Habits reveal themselves over time.

No one is watching now.

That is not a disadvantage.

It is the opportunity to build discipline that lasts.

Chapter 29: Redefining Winning After the Uniform Comes Off

For most athletes, winning was clearly defined.

Scoreboards told the story. Rankings mattered. Results were visible and immediate. You always knew where you stood. You knew when you were ahead and when you were behind. You knew what a good week looked like and what a bad one felt like. Feedback was constant, public, and undeniable.

Then sports end.

And that clarity disappears.

There is no scoreboard in adult life. No rankings posted after a workweek. No judges handing out scores for effort, discipline, or consistency. No whistle that tells you when you are slipping or when you are improving. Without clear markers, many former athletes start searching for substitutes for winning.

That is where problems begin.

Status replaces performance.

Appearances replace progress.

The shift is subtle, but it is powerful.

Why the Loss of a Scoreboard Is So Disorienting

Athletes are conditioned to measure themselves.

You were trained to evaluate performance objectively. You knew the standard. You knew the goal. You knew when you met it and when you did not. That feedback loop shaped behavior automatically. You adjusted without needing motivation because the data was obvious.

When that disappears, the brain still wants feedback.

So it looks for what is easiest to measure.

Titles. Income. Lifestyle. Recognition. External validation.

These become the new scoreboards, not because they are accurate, but because they are visible.

Why Chasing Status Replaces Chasing Performance

Sports reward performance.

Life often rewards appearance.

When performance metrics are unclear, status markers rush in to fill the gap. Job titles. Promotions. Salary numbers. Houses. Cars. Travel. These are easy to see, easy to compare, and easy to broadcast. They feel like progress even when they are not aligned with long-term stability, health, or fulfillment.

In cheer terms, this is focusing on uniforms instead of execution.

The team looks sharp. The branding is clean. The music hits. But underneath, the fundamentals are weak. Timing is off. Conditioning is lacking. Confidence is fragile.

Status is easy to measure externally.

Performance requires internal standards.

Without self-defined criteria, it becomes easy to mistake motion for progress and visibility for success.

Why Status Is So Addictive After Sports

Status provides quick feedback.

You get a raise. You feel successful.

You buy something new. You feel ahead.

You get recognition. You feel validated.

These signals mimic the dopamine of winning competitions. They feel familiar. They feel earned. But unlike athletic performance, they are often disconnected from long-term outcomes.

Status does not ask whether you are stable.

Status does not ask whether you are fulfilled.

Status does not ask whether the path you are on fits your values.

It only asks whether others can see you moving.

That is a dangerous substitute for real progress.

Income vs Fulfillment

Income matters.

It creates options. It provides stability. It reduces stress. It allows you to plan, protect, and invest. Pretending income does not matter is unrealistic and irresponsible.

But income alone does not guarantee fulfillment.

Many people hit income goals and still feel unsettled. They earn more, but feel less connected. They upgrade lifestyle, but lose clarity. They are busy, but not satisfied.

In cheer terms, this is hitting difficulty without joy.

The routine technically works. The skills are there. The score is fine. But something feels off. The performance lacks flow. Confidence feels forced. The reason you started doing the sport gets lost.

Fulfillment comes from alignment.

When effort, values, and goals point in the same direction, progress feels meaningful. When they do not, success feels hollow, even if it looks impressive from the outside.

The Trap of Titles, Houses, Cars, and Comparison

Comparison never stops.

Social media. Coworkers. Friends. Family expectations. These constantly signal what success is supposed to look like. These signals are loud, repetitive, and persuasive.

They push people into decisions that do not fit their actual lives.

In cheer terms, this is copying another team's routine without understanding their strengths.

The choreography might be impressive. The difficulty might be high. But execution suffers because it was never designed for you. Your team's timing is different. Your conditioning is different. Your goals are different.

External validation creates pressure.

Internal alignment creates confidence.

Chasing someone else's version of success almost always leads to regret, resentment, or burnout.

Why Former Athletes Are Especially Vulnerable to Comparison

Athletes grow up in comparison-driven environments.

Rankings. Scores. Rosters. Starting positions. You were constantly measured against others. That environment trains your brain to look outward for feedback.

After sports, that instinct does not disappear.

Without a clear internal scoreboard, comparison fills the void. You measure yourself against peers instead of against your own standards. That leads to decisions driven by optics instead of intention.

Comparison does not ask whether a decision fits your life.

It only asks whether it looks impressive next to someone else's.

What Success Actually Looks Like in Your 30s and 40s

Success evolves.

In early adulthood, success often looks like momentum and recognition. Promotions. Raises. Being busy. Being seen as "going somewhere." That phase is not wrong. It is developmental.

But over time, the definition shifts.

Success becomes about control and stability.

Time flexibility.

Health.

Strong relationships.

Financial breathing room.

Peace of mind.

In cheer terms, this is veteran leadership.

Clean execution matters more than flash. Efficiency matters more than intensity. Consistency matters more than difficulty. You care less about impressing and more about sustaining performance.

Redefining success early prevents burnout and resentment later.

Why Many People Feel Lost Even When They "Win"

This is one of the most confusing experiences former athletes face.

They do what they were told would bring success.

They work hard.

They advance.

They earn more.

And yet, something feels off.

That disconnect usually comes from chasing someone else's scoreboard.

If success is defined externally, it will always move. There will always be someone ahead. Always a bigger title. Always a nicer lifestyle. Always a new comparison point.

Internal definitions create stability. External definitions create treadmill living.

Building a New Scoreboard

Without a scoreboard, you must create one.

This is not optional. If you do not define success intentionally, you will absorb someone else's definition by default.

A personal scoreboard might include:

Savings progress.

Debt reduction.

Work-life balance.

Stress levels.

Health consistency.

Alignment with values.

Time spent on what matters.

These are measurable if you choose to measure them.

In cheer terms, this is setting your own judging criteria.

You decide what counts.

You decide what matters.

You decide how performance is evaluated.

A personal scoreboard creates clarity.

Clarity creates discipline.

Without clarity, effort becomes scattered and motivation becomes unstable.

Why Internal Metrics Feel Uncomfortable at First

Internal scoreboards do not provide instant validation.

No one claps when you reduce debt.

No one posts your improved stress level.

No one congratulates you for choosing balance over optics.

That silence can feel unsettling at first, especially for athletes used to visible feedback.

But that discomfort is a signal you are doing something different.

You are building something sustainable instead of performative.

Coach's Perspective on Redefining Winning

A coach would challenge you directly.

Define winning for yourself.

Stop chasing someone else's scoreboard.

Measure what actually matters.

Stay disciplined even when no one is watching.

Coaches know that the most dangerous moment is when an athlete loses clarity about what winning actually is. Confusion leads to forced effort. Forced effort leads to mistakes.

Clarity drives consistency.

Game Situations and Decision Points

Redefining success shows up in quiet decisions.

You feel behind. Do you compare or redefine success?

You reach a goal. Do you ask whether it actually matters?

You feel pressure to upgrade. Do you pause or react?

You feel busy. Do you ask whether you are progressing or just moving?

Winning is self-defined now.

No one else can do this for you.

Common Athlete Mistakes and Financial Parallels

Athletes chase recognition.

Financially, that leads to overspending and lifestyle inflation.

Athletes confuse motion with progress.

Financially, that leads to misaligned goals and burnout.

Athletes avoid reflection because it feels uncomfortable.

Financially, that leads to drifting through major life decisions.

The pattern is consistent.

When the scoreboard disappears, confusion fills the gap unless you replace it intentionally.

Why Reflection Is the New Competition

Reflection feels passive to athletes.

It does not look like effort. It does not feel intense. It does not create adrenaline. But reflection is how alignment is built.

Asking the right questions replaces chasing the wrong wins.

What actually matters to me now?

What does stability look like in this season of life?

What am I optimizing for?

What am I sacrificing without realizing it?

These questions are uncomfortable, but they are powerful.

Winning the Long Game

Redefining winning creates freedom.

When success is measured internally, financial decisions become intentional instead of reactive. Progress becomes meaningful instead of performative. Confidence replaces comparison because you are no longer competing on someone else's field.

The scoreboard did not disappear.

You just have to build your own now.

Athlete Takeaways

Winning is no longer defined for you.

Status is not performance.

Income matters, but fulfillment matters too.

Comparison distorts decision-making.

Success evolves with life stages.

Internal scoreboards create clarity and confidence.

You spent years training to win on someone else's scoreboard.

Now the challenge is greater.

Define your own.

Chapter 30: Staying Connected Without Living in the Past

Cheer does not just take time and energy.

It shapes identity.

For years, your schedule, friendships, goals, and sense of purpose were built around the team. Practices, competitions, travel, and shared pressure created a tight bond. That environment made effort feel natural because you were never doing it alone.

When cheer ends, that structure disappears fast.

What replaces it is not obvious, and that is where many former athletes struggle.

The Role of Community, Mentorship, and New Locker Rooms

Community is not optional for long-term success.

Athletes are wired for shared effort. Accountability feels easier when someone else is showing up too. Encouragement feels different when it comes from people who understand discipline and sacrifice.

After cheer, you need new locker rooms.

These might be coworkers, professional peers, fitness groups, mentors, alumni networks, or purpose-driven communities. They do not need to look like your old team, but they must serve the same function.

In cheer terms, this is rebuilding the environment that supports consistency. You are not recreating the past. You are building a new structure that fits your current life.

Mentors matter here. Coaches once provided perspective and correction. Mentors fill that role later. They help you see beyond the moment and avoid mistakes you cannot yet see.

Why Isolation Hits Former Athletes Hard

Isolation feels heavier for athletes than for most people.

You are used to feedback. Used to shared struggle. Used to someone noticing when you show up or do not. When that disappears, effort feels invisible.

Invisible effort is harder to sustain.

In cheer terms, this is training alone without mirrors, music, or teammates. You can still work, but motivation drops faster and doubt creeps in.

Isolation often leads to drifting habits. Skipped workouts. Avoided planning. Delayed decisions. Not because you do not care, but because no one is reinforcing direction.

Connection restores momentum.

Finding Purpose Without the Team

Purpose used to be scheduled.

You did not have to search for it. Practice times told you where to be. Competitions told you what mattered. After cheer, purpose must be chosen intentionally.

This is uncomfortable at first.

Many former athletes wait for purpose to appear instead of building it. That waiting often turns into frustration.

In cheer terms, this is standing on the mat waiting for music that is not coming. You have to press play yourself.

Purpose is built through action. Trying new roles. Setting personal goals. Committing to something that matters now, not something that mattered before.

Clarity follows movement, not the other way around.

Healthy Nostalgia vs Being Stuck

Nostalgia is natural.

Cheer was meaningful. It shaped who you are. Remembering those years with pride is healthy. The problem comes when nostalgia becomes comparison.

If your present life is constantly measured against your cheer years, nothing feels good enough. The past becomes the standard, and the present feels like a letdown.

In cheer terms, this is replaying old routines instead of practicing new ones.

Healthy nostalgia honors the experience without anchoring identity to it. Being stuck happens when identity stops evolving.

The goal is appreciation, not attachment.

Creating a Forward-Looking Identity

You did not lose your identity when cheer ended.

You lost a role.

The traits that made you successful did not disappear. Discipline. Commitment. Attention to detail. Team awareness. Pressure management. Those skills are still there.

They now apply to different arenas.

In cheer terms, this is learning a new routine with the same fundamentals. The counts change. The environment changes. The athlete does not.

A forward-looking identity asks different questions.

Who am I becoming now?

What am I building next?

Where do my strengths belong today?

Identity grows when you allow it to evolve.

Coach's Perspective

A coach would not let you isolate.

Find your people.

Stay engaged.

Honor the past without living there.

Build the next chapter with intention.

Athletes grow best in environments that challenge and support them.

Game Situations and Decision Points

You feel disconnected. Do you withdraw or seek community?

You miss the team. Do you appreciate it or compare everything to it?

You feel unsure of direction. Do you wait or take action?

Connection determines momentum.

Common Athlete Mistakes and Financial Parallels

Athletes isolate after sports.

Financially, that leads to drifting habits.

Athletes cling to past identity.

Financially, that leads to decisions based on image instead of alignment.

Athletes avoid new environments.

Financially, that leads to limited growth and opportunity.

Winning the Long Game

Staying connected is not about reliving the past.

It is about building support systems that fit who you are now and who you are becoming. Community, mentorship, and purpose protect discipline when motivation fades.

Strong finishes are never solo.

Athlete Takeaways

- Community supports accountability and consistency.
- Isolation weakens discipline over time.
- Purpose must be built intentionally after sports.
- Nostalgia should inspire, not trap.
- Identity evolves forward, not backward.

Glossary of Cheer and Financial Terms

Glossary of Cheer and Financial Terms

Asset Allocation

Financial Definition:

The way money is divided among different investment types such as stocks, bonds, and cash to balance risk and return.

Cheer Comparison:

How weight and responsibility are distributed across a routine. Too much difficulty without balance causes instability. Proper allocation keeps the routine upright and repeatable.

Assets

Financial Definition:

Things you own that have value, such as cash, investments, real estate, or retirement accounts.

Cheer Comparison:

Your strengths as an athlete. Skills, flexibility, timing, and experience all contribute to the routine's success.

Bonds

Financial Definition:

Loans made to governments or companies that pay interest and return principal over time.

Cheer Comparison:

The base of a stunt. Not flashy, but essential for stability and safety when pressure increases.

Budget

Financial Definition:

A plan for how income is allocated toward expenses, savings, and goals.

Cheer Comparison:

Practice counts. Without knowing the counts, timing falls apart. A budget keeps money moving on rhythm.

Cash Flow

Financial Definition:

Money coming in versus money going out.

Cheer Comparison:

Energy management during a routine. If you burn too much early, you struggle to finish strong.

Compounding

Financial Definition:

Earnings that generate additional earnings over time.

Cheer Comparison:

Muscle memory built through reps. Each rep makes the next one easier and more effective.

Credit

Financial Definition:

The ability to borrow money with the promise of repayment.

Cheer Comparison:

Trust. When earned and managed well, it allows progression. When abused, it leads to instability.

Debt

Financial Definition:

Money borrowed that must be repaid, often with interest.

Cheer Comparison:

Added weight in a stunt. Some weight is manageable. Too much creates risk and strain.

Diversification

Financial Definition:

Spreading investments across different assets to reduce risk.

Cheer Comparison:

Not relying on one athlete to carry the routine. Shared responsibility keeps the team steady.

Emergency Fund

Financial Definition:

Savings set aside for unexpected expenses.

Cheer Comparison:

Spotters. You hope you never need them, but when something goes wrong, they prevent a fall.

ETF (Exchange-Traded Fund)

Financial Definition:

A fund that holds many investments and trades like a stock.

Cheer Comparison:

A full team routine instead of a solo. The system spreads risk and responsibility.

Fees / Expense Ratios

Financial Definition:

Costs associated with managing investments.

Cheer Comparison:

Sloppy transitions. They may seem small, but they drain momentum over time.

Growth Investing

Financial Definition:

Investing in companies expected to grow faster than average.

Cheer Comparison:

Higher difficulty. Potentially higher scores, but requires stronger fundamentals.

Insurance

Financial Definition:

Protection against financial loss from unexpected events.

Cheer Comparison:

Safety mats. You do not perform without them when risk increases.

Liquidity

Financial Definition:

How easily money can be accessed without penalty or delay.

Cheer Comparison:

Flexibility in a routine. When something changes, you can adjust without collapsing.

Net Worth

Financial Definition:

Assets minus liabilities.

Cheer Comparison:

Overall routine score. Not just one stunt, but the full performance evaluated together.

Rebalancing

Financial Definition:

Adjusting investments back to their intended mix over time.

Cheer Comparison:

Mid-season corrections. You fix timing and spacing before small issues become big problems.

Risk

Financial Definition:

The chance that outcomes differ from expectations, including loss.

Cheer Comparison:

Difficulty selection. Higher difficulty increases reward and the chance of mistakes.

Roth IRA

Financial Definition:

A retirement account where money grows tax-free if rules are followed.

Cheer Comparison:

Front-loaded effort. You work harder early so the finish is cleaner later.

Stocks

Financial Definition:

Ownership shares in a company.

Cheer Comparison:

Flyers. They drive growth and excitement but need support to stay in the air.

Tax-Advantaged Accounts

Financial Definition:

Accounts that provide tax benefits, such as retirement plans.

Cheer Comparison:

Structured training. There are rules, but the system improves outcomes when followed.

Volatility

Financial Definition:

Short-term ups and downs in market value.

Cheer Comparison:

A wobble. Normal movement that does not end the routine unless you panic.

Permanent Loss

Financial Definition:

Money that cannot recover due to poor decisions or panic.

Cheer Comparison:

A fall. Often caused by reacting emotionally instead of trusting fundamentals.

Total Return

Financial Definition:

Investment return from both price growth and income like dividends.

Cheer Comparison:

Full routine score. Execution, difficulty, and transitions all matter.

Value Investing

Financial Definition:

Investing in companies believed to be undervalued.

Cheer Comparison:

Clean execution. Less flash, more control, consistent results.

Yield

Financial Definition:

Income generated from an investment, such as interest or dividends.

Cheer Comparison:

Consistent scoring. Not dramatic, but reliable.

Final Note

This glossary exists to reinforce one idea:

Financial concepts become clearer when you understand their role, not just their definition.

Just like cheer, success comes from timing, balance, trust, and repetition.

Disclaimers

Educational Purposes Only

This book is for educational purposes only.

The information provided in *Cheer Money 101* is intended to help readers understand general financial concepts using cheer-based analogies. It does not provide individualized financial, investment, tax, legal, or insurance advice.

Every financial situation is different. Your goals, income, family circumstances, risk tolerance, and time horizon are unique. What works for one person may not be appropriate for another.

Not Financial, Investment, or Legal Advice

Nothing in this book should be interpreted as a recommendation to buy, sell, or hold any specific investment, financial product, or strategy.

This book does not replace advice from qualified professionals, including:

- Financial advisors
- Accountants or tax professionals
- Attorneys
- Insurance professionals

Before making financial decisions, readers should consult professionals who can evaluate their individual circumstances.

No Guarantees or Promises of Results

All investing involves risk, including the possible loss of principal.

Past performance does not guarantee future results. Markets fluctuate. Economic conditions change. Outcomes cannot be predicted or guaranteed.

Examples and scenarios in this book are illustrative only and may not reflect actual results or real-world outcomes.

Tax and Legal Information

Any discussion of taxes, retirement accounts, estate planning, or legal structures is general in nature.

Tax laws and regulations change frequently and vary by jurisdiction. Legal requirements differ based on location and personal circumstances.

Readers should seek personalized tax or legal advice before acting on any information related to these topics.

Athlete and Career Considerations

This book discusses financial topics as they relate to athletes and former athletes, including career transitions and income changes.

It does not provide career placement services, employment advice, or guarantees related to income, compensation, or career success.

Use of Analogies

Cheer and sports analogies are used to make financial concepts easier to understand.

These analogies are educational tools only and should not be interpreted literally. Financial decisions require analysis beyond analogy.

Personal Responsibility

By reading this book, you acknowledge that:

- You are responsible for your own financial decisions
- You understand that financial outcomes involve uncertainty
- You agree to seek appropriate professional guidance when needed

Education improves decision-making, but responsibility remains with the individual.

Contact Information

If you would like to learn more about the concepts discussed in this book or explore additional educational resources, Pat Brown can be found through public platforms including LinkedIn, Twitter, or via a Google search.

For questions specifically related to *Cheer Money 101*, you may contact Pat Brown at:

info@cheermoney101.com

Final Reminder

Financial success is built over time through discipline, planning, and consistency.

This book provides a framework, not a guarantee.

Use it as a guide, not a substitute for professional advice.

Pat Brown OLB, University of Kansas

Made in the USA
Monee, IL
04 November 2026

67387587R00128